The Open Door

By

Neatris C. Mitchell

ISBN: 0-7596-9760-4 (e-book)
ISBN: 0-7596-9761-2 (Paperback)

Library of Congress Number 2002091221

This book is printed on acid free paper.

Printed in the United States of America
Bloomington, IN

1stBooks – rev. 07/13/02

This warm hearted memoir depicting the struggle and eventual success of one woman is timely in that the stories of refugees seeking to make the United States their home is becoming so much a part of our everyday lives. In **THE OPEN DOOR**, Author Neatris Mitchell takes us on her journey from a poor upbringing in Jamaica to success in the media fields here in the U.S.

Rarely is a book written in autobiographical format distinctive and compelling enough to be interesting to those outside the Author`s immediate circle of family and friends. Yes with vivid descriptions, emotionally evocative dialogue, and a certain flair for histrionics Ms. Mitchell portrays her every personal struggle against the overlying theme of this being a struggle we must face at some point in our lives.

Against such a backdrop, the Author sets forth her unabashed faith in God as being the guiding light in her life. She relates this faith to all walks of her life, and depends on this power of the Lord to see her through. While the reader will be fascinated by the many obstacles Ms. Mitchell and her family encounter during their growing up period, he or she will also be engrossed by the Author undying determination, an effect which will captivate even the hard-hearted reader

This is revealing autobiography, one in which those forces that helped shape Neatris Mitchell`s character and personality are highlighted. The Author writes with a sense of humor and paints expressive portraits of herself and of many other colorful personalities she encounters along the way.

Highly recommended for its human drama, the valuable information it imparts and its warm, glowing appeal, **THE OPEN DOOR**, by Neatris C. Mitchell is a must read for all adventures, and keepers of the faith.

<u>Neatris Castoria Mitchell</u>
N.C.Mitchell

INTRODUCTION

"THE OPEN DOOR" (MY GOD IS ABLE)

I was born on the 14th day of April 1939, in the district of maroon town, in the parish of St. James, on the island of Jamaica, West Indies. This district in which I was born, has a historical background. Jamaica, is one of the most beautiful, hard to make it, free and fruitful island of the world.

Since the days of our fore, fathers, man and women have learned to live and toil for what they want, on this island, and because of this, the natives have learned, to love the better things of life, to aim high, and reach out for a place in this world, and most of the people, try to prepare for a place in the world to come.

I n spite of the hard days, or happy and the excited life, of yours and mine, God is able to open and close the widest doors in our lives. Yes! My God is able.

MY NATURAL PARENTS

My parents were not born in the district of Maroon Town, but in a place called St. Elizabeth. They left from St. Elizabeth one morning while it was still dawn to travel to the district of Maroon Town to make a new life. When I visit St. Elizabeth, I found it to be a very fruitful part of the island. This is where most of the Corn, Peas, Mangoes, Breadfruit, Pimento and Aeschylean, come from, to supply other parts of the island and mostly those in the Cities, namely Kingston and Montego Bay.

My mother was born a talented and attractive lady. She was the last of five sisters for her mother and the only daughter for her father who also had two sons, Sam and John. She was 5 feet and 4 inches tall.

My father was of short status, dresses well and always looking neat, with neatly shaped whiskers, thick eyebrow and a nose that was so straight, it looks like an arrow. He was the first of four brothers but the smallest in size, weighing 130 pounds. My father went to Panama, where he worked for a while on the Panama Canal and was soon able to help his younger brothers.

My mother and father built a lovely home, ran a prosperous business and soon they were able to live independently and provide many people in that district with jobs. They gave whatever they could to help the poorer people, who needed help and surely God blessed them. Yes! God was very good to them and before long, they were able to enjoy some of the better things of life, that life had to offer them in those days. Until this day some of those people will tell you, how good my parents were, everyone you meet will say that, even if they had only heard that from others.

The plot of land, my parents, owned, was very fruitful and many of the things purchased by others could be

1

obtained from their cultivation. The land measured 11 acres. On it was found a beautiful and well-kept home. The land of flowers, would find its way into ones heart, and before long, his time would be taken up in gazing at these unusual and beautiful and as attractive as could be. Many people thought they were not permitted to come through the gate but they were wrong because the ones who tried always welcomed in this home.

My parents met at an early age and developed a caring for each other from their parents were journeying from St. Elizabeth to Maroon Town. One day as my mother's parents were on their long journey from one district to the next, the truck in which they were traveling began to give some trouble. As they pull over to the side of the road, the parents of my father saw that they were having some trouble and pulled over too and gave them some help. Strange enough they were going in the same direction and in search of the same things that life have to offer. The two children smiled at each other while their parents try to correct the problem that my grand father was having with his truck.

They were always remembering each other long after they parted until one day strange but true they met again in Maroon Town into a grocery store. Excitement filed the air and they wanted to see more of each other.

Eutace: "Which way do you go"

Ivy: "I am going that way"

Eutace: "I am happy to know that you are going my way" My name is Eustace what is yours

Ivy   "my name is Ivy and I just moved here with my parents from St. Elizabeth. I am happy too that you are going my way.

Eustace: "I have always remembered you since our parents met that day while fixing that truck."

Ivy   "My home is around the corner, close to the Reservoir. Do you know where?"

Eustace: "Sure!" I passed by that way about a week ago. Well I have to be going this way, but I hope to be seeing much more of you."

SUCH EXCITEMENT

Eustace was so excited, and he could not hold his excitement at dinner

Eustace: "I have met a beautiful girl today. She is the most beautiful girl I have ever seen. She is a dressmaker, she sings the lead for the church choir and she is going to be in concerts too."

Mother: "Where is she living."

Eustace: "She lives close to the Reservoir, her parents donated the property to the Government, for the people of this district to have water. I would love to have all of you meet her."

Eustace: "May I invite Ivy over on Sunday?" ***(Eustace ask his mother as she stirred the red peas soup.)***

Mother: "You ask that question when everyone is at the dinner table my son."

Eustace: "Dad, may I invite the young lady that I was talking about for dinner on Sunday? I really want everyone to meet her dad."

Dad: "Are you sure that is what you want to do son?"

Eustace: "Maybe next Sunday"

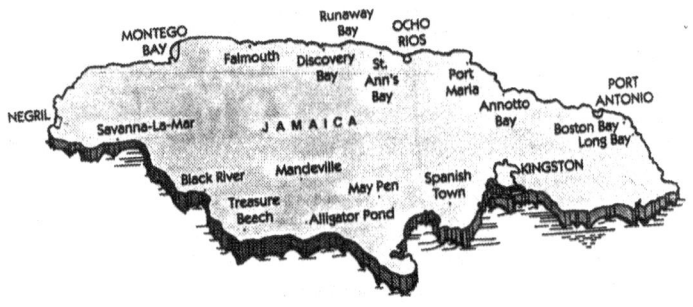

The family of Eustace was pleased to have Ivy and her parents over

They had a good time.

Ivy: "I shell ask my parents to have you and your family over next Sunday
Will you join us?"

Dad: "Why not? We certainly enjoy having you here. Our son has good taste He is certainly a branch of the old tree." (Big laugh)

Mother of Ivy "So Eustace, what do you think of my daughter? You seem like a nice young man."

Eustace: "I would love to marry her, may I? I know she is not ready but I will wait for her."

Ivy: "I will be happy to tell, but I must think it over."

Father of Eustace: "We have had a wonderful time, we must be leaving now. Thanks for everything."

Eustace pleased that he came and very happy for such warm welcome

The night each time Eustace turned, he thought about Ivy.

Eustace: "I just came by to walk you apart of the way, if you do not mind"

Ivy: "Why would you want to give yourself all that trouble?"

Ivy was very happy he came but held on tightly to her excitement towards Eustace.

Eustace: "One day I would like you to meet my parents and I meet your parents"

Ivy: "What! My parents? Oh no! Why would you want to meet my parents? I don`t think I would want you meet them ever"

Eustace: "I would tell them that I think I like you and that if all work well, I may some day marry you, young lady"

Ivy: "Oh! No! Sir! I do not want to get marry as yet. I am too young."
I have a lot things to do before I get around to marring anyone."

Eustace: "What would you like to do before you get married?"

Ivy: "I have a lot of things to learn about how to be a good wife and mother and how to share the spending load and live a happy life, my dear."

Eustace: "I would wait for as long as you want me to."

Ivy: "Now you have a good day I will be seeing you again."

They parted and each went in a different direction to work. Eustace and Ivy began to see each other more often until finally both of their parents met. It was a happy meeting. Than one day the wedding date was set. Both sides eager to see them join hands in marriage and to wish them a happy life ever after.

Ivy: I am so sleepy in the morning and nausea too. I must go to the see doctor.

Eustace: Ok, I will go with you in the morning.

Doctor: "What seem to be the problem Ms. Smith."

Ms. Smith: "I am so nauseous in the days Doctor."

Doctor: "You are going to have a baby *(Doctor talking to Mr. and Ms. Smith)*

Nurse: "You got a girl."

Eustace   "Darling you got your wish, a girl."

Ivy: *(Smiling turned over in her bed and faced the wall)* "I am so happy, for her but I am so tired. This will be the best loved child in the world."

Ivy: I am having some of those nauseous feelings I had before Castoria was born. "I wonder if I am expecting a son this time?"

Eustace: Doctor is my wife expecting a baby? I would love to have a son this time. *(All smiling)*

Doctor: "Yes! She is, lets hope it is a son."

Eustace: "I am almost out of material, I must leave to get fresh supplies tomorrow. You don`t have that baby until I return. *(Ivy laughing said: believe me I will wait for you.)*"

Ivy: "My husband left two days ago to get some supplies, but did not return home. Please find him."

Sheriff: "We will try our best, mam. You take it easy."

Soon they would not be around much longer, for by the time I was six years old, and my brother was ready to be born. My father had died and was ready to be buried on his own land where some cocoa tree had grown, making it a nicely shade area where the flowers grow tall and bloom their beautiful petals. The doctors were puzzled about his death, but no one bothered to get to the bottom of what caused his death. Now we were left to a merciful God, and a loving mother. Yes! It was not much longer when my mother was snatched away by the cold hand of death.

John: What about the will my brother left for us?

Ivy: Well my husband did not make a will for us. We thought it was just too early for that, but we were so wrong.

Miss Paterson: Ms. Smith your husband is the father of my son.

Ivy: What! Are you serious?

Miss Paterson: Yes! Mam

Ivy: Why did you not tell me this long ago?

Miss P: Well Mam, he said he told me to drop it right there, he said he could not face the public with such shameful things.

Ivy: I can hardly believe what I am hearing. Miss P, I hate to be mixed up in these things but I will do what I can to help. What is the name of the child?

Miss P: His name is Ashley.

Ivy: For the child sake, I will do what I can to help in taking care of his needs. I do not want him to live in wants because of his parents mistake... My God, who in this world can you trust?

Miss P.   Thanks a lot Mrs. Smith, this is a relief.

Ms. Smith: This is realy a shock for me. I never believe my husband would fool around. What in the world did they have in common.

Simon: Don't even question that baby, Eustace told me about him.

Ivy: Oh my Lord!

Simon:	I have found a buyer for the business. The price is good. He can pay for it and take it over in two weeks, if you so desire.
Ivy:	I do appreciate all the things you are doing. You can have him occupy the place, as early as possible.

After the death of my mother things slowly began to change. My mother began to worry and property became of less value to her. Then on the last day of March, the day I became nine years old, my mother was too weak to hold and kiss me the next day at 11am., she died. The doctor said she was sick with her heart. Everyone who knew my parents mourned for them. Thanks to those wonderful people.

Ivy:	Simon, please rush for the midwife, I think I am ready to have the baby.
Simon:	I will leave right away.
Midwife:	Yes Ms. Smith, you are ready to have your baby.

Within a short time the baby was born.

Nurse:	Well Ms. Smith you have a son.
Ms. Smith:	A son? Oh! Thank God. This is the best gift I could ever receive. That his father died eight days ago. Yes! Just days before he was born, I hope he will follow in the good steps of his father.
Nurse:	Miss Ivy, some family members are here to visit.

| Ms. Smith: | Please have them come in. Hi! Folks, it is so good to see you. I have a son his name is Haden. I am sorry his father is not here to hold him. |

Soon Ivy was home to take care of a son and a daughter, all without a husband.

| Ms. Smith: | Things have not been going well since the death of my husband. I know you are doing your best, but none of us can do it. The way my husband Eustace did it. It seem that we must sell all that we can sell at this time. |

(Brothers are talking among themselves.)

| John: | Folks, I am asking you again, what about the will my brother left for… when do we get our share? |

| Ivy: | Young men, Let us all get together and settle everything now, once and for all. I would like everyone to be happy, and to be at peace now once and for all. I would like to be happy, and to be at peace with each other. Come guys let us sit here. (Every ones face was beaming with joy.) Suddenly, Ivy was not feeling well luckily the sharing was already done. |

| Ivy: | Simon! said Ivy, "Please rush me to the doctor, I am not felling well." |

Simon:	"I will leave right away." I will try to get you there as quickly as possible.
Doctor:	Ms. Smith, "You are worrying too much, worrying is not good for you. You must be around to take care of the children, so you have to cheer up my dear."
Willy	How much did each of us get from the eleven acres of land that was shared?
Simon:	' Who are the children going to stay with?"
John:	"Their aunt I guess."
Aunt:	"Since there is no one else to take them, I will do so. I will pack their things and take them with me today."
Simon:	"My wife is too busy to take care of them."
John:	"I have enough children at my home, so there is no room for them."

Said John as he moves his head from side to side.

Willy:	"My home is not big enough to keep them."
Aunt:	"I do not know why I have to take both of you when nothing was shared for me. You are just going to have to work your way through life."
Aunt`s Husband	"How are you young lady?"
Castoria:	"I am fine Sir."

Aunt`s Husband   "How old are you now?"

Castoria: "I am nine years old sir."

Husband: "You and your brother will be living with us for a long time, so make yourself at home, we will take good care of you."

Aunt: "Well children! Here we go to church on Saturdays as the Bible says, we keep the Sabbath. We do not go on Sundays like your parents."

Thauntan: "Yes we can go with you on Saturdays and go to our church on Sundays."

Aunt: "No dear! Saturdays only."

Castoria: "Yes aunt, we will go with you on Saturdays."

Aunt: "Costoria! You will have to wash the clothes and help with the baking and cooking too. We have a lot to do here so make yourself useful, my child."

Castoria: "I will do what you ask, Mam."

Thauntan: "When is mama coming back? I want her to come back now."

Castoria: "She will not be coming back, this is our home now. Please do not cry."

DAYS OF TROUBLE

When my brother and I were born to the family we were very happy received but now things were different. Now the time of trouble started for my brother and I. We had no one to live with and each relative said they could not take us because nothing was left for them to use to take care of us. This was no fault of my parents excepting that they did die at an early age. They were hard-working people who left us eleven acres of land, well cultivated, a beautiful home, prosperous business and money in the bank.

Sure enough my uncles had their share. Each took an amount that satisfied his desire. A portion was also given to a brother whom my mother knew after the death of my father. My father was a very well- respected man of business and money and never let such things as a child out of his home and with another woman reach the eyes and ears of the public, even if it should cost him his life. My mother trying to hold the high standard of my father did all she could to make that other woman and child live a comfortable life. She said "My father was a great husband and father who made mistakes like other men do."

after we were raffled for, like a deck of cards, we were pitted by one of my mother`s sisters. I must tell you how much I appreciate her kindness to us. We were never hungry or naked, and each day she showed us how to walk in the way of the Lord. The things I learnt then, have ben keeping me all of these years. This aunt that had pity on us was not very friendly with my mother, and now it was her chance to reveal her feelings for us and surely this was done to the full length with explanation what the problem was. This was a heavy load for her husband and herself. Lucky for us, inflation was not too much in this Island at this time. Her husband who did not do too much talking was ready and willing to help us. He was born into the Seventh Day

Adventist Religion and so like a teacher, he was able to explain the writing of Mrs. E. White and the Prophetic Writing of the Bible, going from Genesis to the Revelations.

STUDY ROOM

MY AUNT`S HUSBAND STUDY ROOM

Now as the years go by and these prophecies are being fulfilled and pointed out that the coming of the Lord and Savior is nearer, I have great rejoicing, I have peace of mind knowing God`s words are true and shall stand forever and not one shall fail. As the months and weeks went by the sorrow for my parents die slowly into the distance I could see hard days ahead.

Aunt: "Castoria you are now in charge of the baking. I will show you how."

Castoria: "How much baking will I do?"

Aunt: "I have three girls who have to go to the three schools to sell lunch to the children, so it need a lot of time."

Castoria: "Will I be able to go to school one day per week?"

Miss Tat: "mother say you should learn sewing with me one hour per day."

Castoria: "I will be happy to do that."

Castoria: "Pastor, I want to be baptized."

Pastor: "Sure little sister. How old are you? Twelve, You could be in the Baptism if you did not have pneumonia."

Castoria:	"Yes, Pastor! I have prayed to God and he will heal me."
Pastor:	"Ok, be ready for Sunday morning."
Miss Tat:	"Tomorrow we are going to the field to plant some cow peas, would you like to come with us?"
Castoria:	"Sure! I would love to see how this is done."
Miss Tat:	"Now you cannot wear those fancy dresses, like you use to." "Now you only wear those dresses to church, this I hope you do understand"
Vee:	"Thauntan, you will have to help with the goats, and fowls and picking up the fire wood. I will teach you how."
Castoria:	"I must wash some clothes today, may I have some please?"
Aunt:	"Yes dear! Wash these sheets well, if not the edge will hold the dirt, they are made from bags that carry flour."
Castoria:	"Oh! This seem like a lot of clothes, do I wash for all nine of us?"
Aunt:	"Oh yes! Just get the brown soap and the scrubbing board and wash them in the big wash pan. Sometimes you can go down to the river and scrub them on the stone and rinse them in oval blue water."

The privilege of a son and daughter, were gone and now we must face the days of a handy man and a maid. My brother was now ready to take care of the goats and cows and clean the yard, bringing the fire wood and do many duties of a farmer. Soon he began to cry for mother and pray to God to let him die. I was still so young but I was able to comfort him by telling him that God loves us and would surely take care of us. Thanks to Ms. White my Sunday School teacher who always drives this in week after week. My work load is heavy too but God was with us each step of the way and we were able to bear it without making a face. I had to wash and cook for this family consisting of nine people. My aunt bake each day and send it to three schools to be sold to the children. Some things were also sold at the business place on the block which she lives. Soon I could do the baking too. We did not live in a fancy house anymore and so cleaning became harder and had to be more often and this was my duty also to see that my aunts children were studying for their examinations and doing other things.

In the country most washing was done by hand at home or the river. There were no powdered soap, brush or liquid bleach to wash with excepting Oval Blue, made of little blocks. These little blocks were diluted and put into the last rinsing water while rinsing is being done in a tub or wash pan as they were called. It was so much harder than the washing of today but the clothes of those days when washed were as white as snow. Seeing I had to get these clothes so clean and doing this with what is called brown soap by the bar my finger began to get sore in the nails and I need not tell you how much pain I had. I had to get them clean or they would be wet and rubbed in the earth and I would still have to wash them.

Some of the clothes that I had to wash day after day

So you see I still had to wash them I could not stop and in spite of all the pain, I had to work on. Not until that day when God change my mortal body into the immoral body, will my nails again be the way they were made. In this country, the children do not have too much time, for one to go to school and so far awhile, I was only able to go one day per week. By the time I was twelve years old, I had to stop completely, and I was out of school for one year. I was told by my aunt that I could not go back, but would have to learn dressmaking.

The dressmaking lesson was given to me from 11:00am to 12:00 noon for four days per week, by my aunt's daughter, who was living in the same house, and who was a dressmaker, I did not like this and neither did I have the time to prepare for the lesson, and soon this dressmaking lesson was brushed aside and was soon forgotten.

MY DECISION

As everyone got, bigger, changes was made, so bright and early one Friday morning, was shipped away in a truck to live with an old lady. This lady was a firm believer in her church, and the Bible, but also believed that Sunday is the Sabbath. This made me very unhappy because of the things she eats, I was uncomfortable with her way of worship, and so I tried very hard to explain to her some of the things I learnt from the Bible, things like the seventh day Sabbath, and that it can be proven from the Bible that it is the Sabbath of the Lord our God. That God`s commandments, stands fast forever and ever.

My aunt thought of a way to the family load so she came up with a plan to send me to live with a lady.

Aunt: "Castoria, I am going to send you to live with an elderly lady who lives alone."

This made Castoria very happy with joy in her heart she anxiously wanted for an answer.

Castoria: "When do I leave."

Aunt: "You should go on Friday so that you can get a ride in Mr. Smith truck. Mrs. Blake will be very happy to have you."

Mrs. Blake: "Do you know how to shop young lady. How about cooking and washing."

Castoria: "Yes I Mam, I can do those things."

24

Castoria: "Mrs. Blake! Is a Sabbath keeping church close by here?"

Mrs. Blake: "Not close and here, you must go on Sundays."

"THE HOLY BIBLE, WITH GOD`S TEN COMMANDMENTS"

Castoria: "Well Miss, I have been studying my Bible with my aunt from Genesis to Revelations say I must go to the Sabbath day."

Mrs. Blake: "Well my dear, you must go on Sunday, that`s it."

Castoria: "Miss! God`s commandments stands fast forever and ever."

Mrs. Blake: "Come my child, let`s get some work done."

Castoria: "Sings Holy Sabbath day of rest."

Aunt and family: "What are you doing here Castoria? What happen?"

Castoria: "I just wanted to be back, I was not happy there."

THE DAY GOD INTERVENED

The   Vaughansfield   Temple

This Sabbath I was able to go to church, since she did not believe so at 6:00pm that evening. I took my suitcase and said goodbye to her. I must tell you that before she died, she became a Seven day Adventist. My young mind was stayed on God, and I remembered how he said, "He cares for the bird of the air, and the lilies of the field, and that I am of more value to him." With this in mind, I went back to join my brother, attend the Seven day Adventist Church, got baptized, and to have God make a way for me. Life became harder, and soon I began to pray without ceasing and surely God heard my cry."

At that time the church in that district, was well attended. The principal who was Mr. C. Jones, was beyond a doubt, a man of God. The life he lived, tells of his connection with the heavenly father. He was a kind, pleasant and jovial person. Full of wisdom, and the things he took time off to teach me, and all the other students, will never be forgotten, and ninety-seven percent of his students has become a success. How much he means to me, eternity alone will be able to tell.

Pauline: "Uncle will be holding a dance on Friday night, would you like to come over? We can dance in our room."

Castoria: "Ok, Pauline, I will stop in to see you, and to see what it is all about, but I do not believe in going to these places."

27

Pauline:	Hello folks, this is the night Castoria is going to dance. I cannot wait to see her dance.
Castoria:	Aunt, can I get ready now, to go over to Pauline?
Aunt:	Yes Castoria, but please be back on time.
Castoria:	Pauline, did you ask me to come to a dance tonight? What kind of music will you be playing here tonight? I will be going home. While there I do my lessons that dancing is not for me. Enjoy yourself, I will see you soon, I will see you tomorrow.
M. V. Leader:	I need someone to read this story, and give it as a talk Castoria, please do it for me. I need it for my meeting this coming Sabbath.

After M.V.Meeting that evening, everyone said it was well done also the visitor who was in charge, of the meeting, and had to plan that evenings program. He asked me for the name of the school that I was attending. It was very embarrassing to say I was out of school, at this age, but how could I lie?

Mr. Rose:	That story was well done tell me: "What school do you attend?"
Castoria:	I have been out of school for about one year now, Sir. Mr. Rose scratches his head.
Mr. Rose:	What! I do not believe it.

Castoria:	Sir, I would love to go back to school even one day per week like I used to.

Mr. Rose:	I must see the school principal to see if there is something he can do for you.

The day following the day I gave the talk, at the M. V. Meeting, was a Sunday, that day, teacher Jones came and asked my aunt to allow me to go back to school.

Teacher:	Hello, aunt, How are you today? "I think you should send Castoria back to school, she has a bright future ahead of her."

Aunt:	"Yes teacher! Only if she can go from 4:00pm to 6:00pm. She cannot go to school, like the other children do because she has a lot of work to do."

Principal:	"Well if that is all she can have, it is better than nothing."

Her answer to him, was a very pleasant one but, that night, as he left, my aunt got into a rage, and accuse me of asking the teacher, to come to her.

Aunt:	"Why did you ask that teacher to ask me to let you go back to school? I did not get anything from your parents, so you just have to work, and go to school and that is just it."

I am so glad he came, so I did not mind, what was said afterwards. The following week I was able to go back to school.

Now I must study for my first examination which had started three months before I went back. How can I now be able to reach up to the level of the others? Well through Christ we can do all things, I still had all my other work to do, while I study for my examination which had started even before I got there.

Now I must go to sleep one o`clock in the mornings, and be up at 4:00 am to study. Seeing that now, I could only go to school, from 4pm to 6pm 4 evenings per week. I go to choir rehersal, two evenings per week. Prayer meeting one evening, and no studying Friday, and Saturday evenings.

Castoria: "Teacher Jones, I I would like to take the exam when the time comes." Can I!, because I started late this caused teacher Jones to be very doubtful about my passing the examination. I could see this as he schratched his head before giving me an answer. So I told him to let me take it on my own. My God was good to me then, and ever after, so so that even until this day, when I started writing to you, I have never experienced a failure. Teacher Jones was kind enough, to sign the forms for me, so that I could go my own way, to take the exam." Nothing that is good for me, I must admit, that it took walking with my books, and constant praying, and crying to God, day and night for help, to bring me success. After passing my exam, I had to go to teacher Jones, 1,2, and 3, times, again, and again, he said yes. Each time he said yes! Castoria, I will do it for you.

Castoria: "Each time I would say, thank you very much Sir."

Jim: "Castoria we are going on a picnic, on Sunday, would you care to go with us?"

Castoria: "Thank you very much," I would love to go, but I have much work to do. I do not have any spare time, between church work, school work, and choir practice, all of my time is taken."

Jim: We are going to the North Coast, "How can you miss it?" "How can you miss up such a trip girl?"

Castoria: "I hope you happy people will have a good time."

Teacher: "Castoria! Your are so sick how can you take this your third year exam you must go to the hospital."

Castoria: "I must go, even if someone, must take me to the exam room. I will go to the hospital whem all of this is over."

Mrs. Spence: "Young lady I noticed that you have been here for the pass 12 days and no one came to visit you."

Castoria: "I have no parents, and my relative, and church members, and other folks, are too far away from here.

Mrs. Spence: "So tell me about yourself Castoria!"

Castoria: "It is a long story! I am now waiting for my exam result, so I can be a teacher."

Mrs. Spence: "I am very happy, to hear that, you could come to live with me. Just just come when you are ready, I will be waiting for you."

Youngman: "Here is a telegram, for one Miss Castoria.

Castoria: "I must have passed my exam! Thank you Lord."

Castoria: ***(Read the telegram) which said, "Your room is ready Castoria, come next Wednesday."***

Soon I was successful with all three of my examinations. I was now able to apply to the government in my country, for a job. Even though I was still too young. I should have told you that before I took my third exam, I got very ill, and fainted twice in the exam room. The following day I had to be taken to the Montego Bay Public Hospital, where I remained for thirteen days here is where I met Mrs. Spence. She is the kind of woman, that every girl would love to have for a mother. She asked me to come and live with her, I did, and she kept her promise. She treated me like her own daughter. When I joined her after passing my exam.

When I went to Mrs. Spence, I was able to sleep in a bed like the one my parents had for me. When I read the telegram that the young man brought me, it said: "Your room is ready, Castoria come next Wednesday." I was very excited!

Mrs. Spence: "Welcome my child.   This is your new home."

Castoria: "Now I must settle down, and enjoy the life that I lost."   This I thought about, as I unpack my things from my small suitcase." I must now work to help my brother, whom I left behind. Soon I was looking for a job.

Castoria: Sir! "I am here to apply for a job. I am applying for a teacher's position."

Principal: "Miss you are so young to be a teacher. We will hire you if the board agrees to do so." We will let you know by mail.

Few days later, the mail came.

Castoria: Mrs. Spence, Hello, I have got a job! Oh yes! I got it."

(Castoria all excited as she ran with letter in hand)

Mrs. Spence is motherly to everyone, and I always pray that God will continue to be good to her and lengthen her days, keep her in good health, and let her life prosper in him. This Mrs. Spence lives in Montego Bay, and since that day I learned to love this place in so much that I have built my home here. No matter where I go, I shall always remember this place.

Yes! There is no secret that my God have for me, that he cannot hold for you. He has taken nothing and made something out of it. He can reach down in the deepest hell and lift the Vilset sinner out from the pit of sin. He can wash your sins away and make you whiter than snow. He is father of the fatherless. He is mother of the motherless. He is shelter to the homeless. Yes! He is light to the blind. He is strength to the weak. Food to the hungry and water to the thirsty. He is the Lilly of the valley. He is bright and morning star. He is the fairest of ten thousand. He is the only pilot who can take you, and I safely from this world to life eternally into the next. He is my savior, will you make him yours.

MY KNIGHT

David: "Hello, young lady you look like someone I have seen before."

Castoria: "What can I do for you?"   *That voice is like David's but it could never be.*

David: "Do you work in this area?"

Castoria: "Just for the summer, I have a long holiday from school and I can use the extra money."

David: "What is your name?"

Castoria: "My name is Castoria, and I have to be going."   *Then she looked up and saw that it was David.*

David: "We have been seeing each other for the past 3 years and six months and you seem like the person I need to be my wife. Will you marry me?"

Castoria: "Yes David!, I will marry you at the end of one year, if you will agree for me to continue my schooling."

Castoria: "I would love to send some application to some nursing schools honey. I do not think you would mind? Do you?"

David: "We will have to find the right person to take care of the children, so we must start looking right away."

Aunt Julie: "Castoria, please meet Beverly. She is to see David but he never came. Poor girl she spent the whole day now she have 18 miles to travel home."

Shirley: "Well I must be leaving now." Bye now Castoria it was nice meeting you."

Castoria: ***With an ugly grin.*** "It was nice meeting you too."

David: "Hi honey, Hello aunt!"

Aunt Julie: "A young lady was here, her name is Shirley."

David: "Why did she come her? Did Castoria see her?"

Aunt Julie: "Oh yes, she did."

David: "Ok, I just thought of some thing good, I will go to his house to find out what is going on."

David: "Castoria after three years of writing letters and seeing each other just once per week while you are busy, I can now see you home from work."

Castoria: "We have been friends for three years and still I have more years of waiting. Nothing can be done before the time."

David: "Why do we still have to wait? I am 22 years old, I have a home, I am a contractor, I am making good money, why do you want to wait?"

Castoria: "We have lots of plans to make for the future. There is no more to life than just material things. We need strong love."

Castoria: "Oh! Marriage! I will marry you. You are handsome witty and prosperous. Why not?"

Castoria: "Have you seen David come by?"

Gardner: "Oh no miss, I have not seen him come by this evening."

Castoria: "Thank you sir, but let me knock on his door."

Castoria: "Thank you sir, but I have to leave."

David: "Honey do you love my outfit? Lets go."

Castoria: "Your outfit darling, please let us walk this evening, it is a nice day."

David: "Why not? Lets go."

C astoria: "It is over for us David, you may have Shirley to be your wife. I know you went

37

to the bus station to see her, too. This is the evening we are walking together for the last time."

David: "What are you talking about? No one can come between us. You should know that."

Castoria: "If a man cannot be faithful before he is married, why do you think he should after the wedding is over? Good-bye darling."

David: "You would never do this to me, three and a half years to go down the drain?"

They then parted and each went his way

David: "Well Castoria, if I am not going to marry you, I will not stand here and watch someone else marry you. It will be better if I leave."

Mrs. Beckers: "Castoria! I do not know what happen, but will you please forgive David."

Mr. Hinds "Miss Castoria, David asked me to speak to you, he wants to know if you will forgive him and marry him. What should I tell him."

Castoria: "I have made up my mind, he can marry someone else."

Mr. Hinds: "Well Castoria, he is leaving next Tuesday."

Miss Lee: "My son is depressed, he is afraid that he is going to loose you."

Castoria: "Why should he? I know Beverly must have had a very good reason to have come this far to see him. It can only be one of us."

THE HAND OF GOD

The hand of God is powerful, it can lead you through the darkest night. It can lift you from the lowest debts, it can life you from the lowest debts, it can guide you over the plains, lift you to the highest height. One day as I was making plans to be baptize there became a harshness in my throat and after which the doctor said I was having pneumonia, and I was baptize, to the amazement of every one present that day. From the moment I came out of the water, I felt better. What am I saying, is that the sickness went, and I did not have to go back for that specific illness. Many years have passed since all of this happened but this which is just one of my experience will not be forgotten. My friends the Lord has done so much for me, much more than I can tell you at this time.

I have always wanted to become a nurse, above everything else, so I decided that now is the time to place my application. My timing was not right, because I was too young, so what I did was become a Junior. Teacher is the meanwhile, while I wait on the years. My time was well spent with the children. The parents appreciated the work I was doing, they cared for me very much. On Friday`s they brought gifts, and none of those gifts were cheap. I was able to learn a lot from the children, as well as the lesson I had to teach them. At that my boyfriend and I were already dating for three years and a half had broken up but sad to say he did not know enough about me to know that some girls will over I will not. Many people thought we were right for each other, but I believe that what a man do before he is married, many times he will do the same things after he is married. The bad habits will turn to worst, and some of the good turn to bad, but the man which strive to be an ideal man, will blossom and bloom, better qualities day after day. I was very sorry about the breaking off, of our engagement, but I feel that was the best time to do this. All the sorrow I had in me, took a long time to go from me, but that was the way it went.

Well two years later a tall handsome one came along, and soon my mind was changed about wanting to live alone. So after we saw other for six months we got married. The hope of becoming a nurse was always in my mind, and so after being blessed with a son and a daughter and my daughter being two years and two days older that my son I was accepted in this school which is the largest in my country`s largest city.

Aunt: "Castoria! How do you like teaching."

Castoria: "Oh, I love it. I have grown to love people. They have interest in their children. They show so much appreciation for the service we give but, soon I will have to leave them to become a nurse.

Aunt: "That`s wonderful."

Castoria: "I hope a reply from my application will arrive soon."

Castoria: "Mrs. Beckers one of the nursing school has accepted my application."

Mrs. Beckers: "Who will take care of the family?"

Castoria: "It is all taken care of."

MY SON AND DAUGHTER

WITH THEIR SITTER

Matron: "Welcome to this training school, Castoria." Why would you want to become a nurse when you have six diplomas to choose other things from?"

Castoria: "I want to be of geater service to humanity."

Mrs. Nelson "I am your brother-in-law's neighbor, did he say so to you?"

Sister Mcfarlene: "Being here is serious business, just keep that in mind.

Sister Nelson: "With hard work and dedication you will achieve your goal."

Castoria: "I shall do my best."

David: "Honey I am calling from work, the children wants you to come home, but they are well taken care of. We are fine."

Castoria: "Hello, David, I shall be home this weekend. See you soon."

David: "We are so happy to see you."

David: "Before you go back to school we must talk. You see we do have a little money, just a little but we must get a home of our own."

Castoria: "Boy this is going to be real hard, but we can build two bedrooms, kitchen and one bath and then we move in. Then we can build little by little."

David: "That is a very good idea."

Castoria: "I will start putting in the money I can earn each week, at school with yours and then we can get started."

David: "Now that we have the idea we can go in search of a beautiful piece of land."

Castoria: "Yes, David where would you like to live?"

David: "Where I can have the sun early mornings, until it sets, the full view of the town, grow lots of fruits, flower trees and vegetables and a lot of room for the children to play."

Castoria: "Aunt, I will be out of school next month, I will be working five minutes from home."

Bertha: "Castoria! A little boy across the road has fallen in a pit. Come! Come! Do something!"

Castoria ran as fast as she could to help he then regained consciousness and was then taken to the hospital for treatment.

I was asked by the person who did the interviewing, why I wanted to be a nurse after having so many trade and profession from which to live and having many job offers and some seem to be much easier jobs? But nursing to me means much more than most things. It was very hard for me to leave my family and to go one hundred and eighteen miles away from home to me it was worth every minute of it. I have had hard days, days when I felt I must give it all up but when a patient says "Thank you" it means so much to me, and it makes life more meaningful. Each day I would pray before I start my day`s task with my patients, and with him by my side I was able to do my work with a smile.

I pray that God would help me to do my best and help, me to bring some comfort to these pepole who are burdened with pain and sores. Each day I try to let them know that sickness will not last forever and some day soon Jesus will come to take this sinful body ours and give us a perfect one, if we surrender our heart to him and if we live for him. That he will not take away our pain because we serve him but we must trust him, even if it permits us to be in pain, and say no, to some of our prayers.

I have seen that my labor is not in vain because men and women have chosen to serve God because of this. I am praying that God will continue to help me as I continue to do what I can to help the human race, and that you may continue to bring men and women the loving message of a soon coming Christ.

My husband and I started with little or no money, after our wedding which was a simple one we had five English pound left in the bank that is less than twenty American dollars in those days but were not owing any bill that had to be paid. Since both of us had no parents because the parents on both sides were already dead. We had no one to help us now we must sail alone lives ocean. Firstly we must work very hard to get a comfortable home. Soon this was

44

done since most of my days were spent in Montego Bay during those days, we love this place so much, we build our first home here. This home is five minutes drive from the midtown of the city. It is sitting on top of a hill a place called Glendevon. In this area lives three classes of people but this did not make much difference, because everyone was nice and friendly. The sun was always shining here, from the early morning until the last, before the night shadows fall. From one of the windows in my bedroom and from the veranda lies the view of the vast town of Montego Bay, with small ships coming in and going out. It was a pleasure to watch their movements some as they *move slowly away gaining more speed as they go along, or getting slower as they coming in to lay down their anchor which can be heard far away when this is done.*

The wind is always blowing gentle and always swaying the branches of the large shade tree in front of the yard. The flowers were carefully planted each one as they are into an apartment by themselves. They would send forth lusty petals all year round. A small bird house was built by the fence that separated my close neighbor's yard from mine. This dog house polished two times weekly and always well kept. The ackee, coconut, avocado, custard apple, sweet sop, breadfruit, cane, banana at the back of the yard and the large shady ginep trees, in the front of the yard, makes this a lovely place to live. The Christmas tree planted by my husband on the other side of the stairway is decorated each Christmas. A nicely built home with most of the necessary comforts, ones like us can afford requires more gratitude to God than we can give. All this and more I must leave to go to a strange land, to meet strange people and little did I know to start a new life.

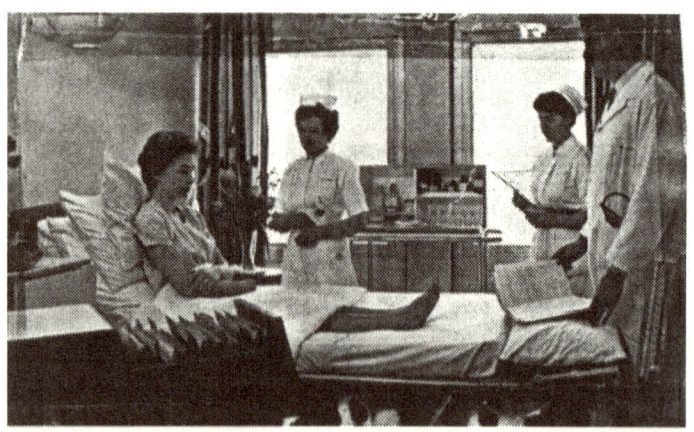

DEEP WATER PAIR

DEEP WATER PAIR IN MONTEGO BAY

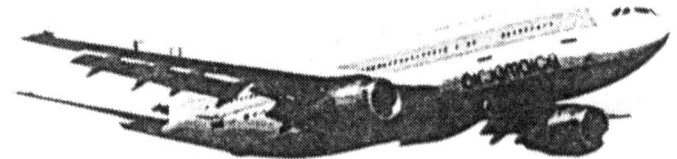

SCENES FROM MONTEGO BAY
JAMAICA W.I.

Lucia: "Castoria! We have voted on having you as a member of our senior choir."

Castoria: "I was so young yet, I would sing with the boys group as well as the girls group and duet too. So Ann you can do it too and you too Lucia."

Ann: "I do not think I would be able to do that. Not me stand before all those people? No sir!"

Castoria: "I received my engagements, oh boy! I had to sing in St. Ann, and Falmouth`s Welcome Hall and many other places, plus the choir and weddings, but I love it."

You see I when I was ten years old, I was asked by my teacher to write a poem. When this was completed and shown to him, he did not believe that I did this by myself. Since this was so, I decided to write verses, about things of life, nature, every-day living, and other things, and soon I was able to use some of these verses for songs. Today I hope my dear teacher will be able to enjoy some of the things I now write. I have now done some writing, some years of nursing, and some years of family life, and now I must along with these things, continue to write songs, and do more singing. I have been singing since I was ten years old. I have been singing in groups, choir and by myself. Oh! Maybe you would like to know how I got started singing by myself.

It happened like this! It was a pleasant evening, and a day the church had set aside for a great evening. People came in by the trucks, cars, buses and on foot until every seat was full. This was a great day for me. Do you know how it is when you are ten and having a day like this, a big day when you would be all dressed up, especially when this do not happen too often. A bigger girl and I, were to do a duet, the big moment came, and the organist was seated, the organ sounded, and off we went, but my partner did not get her pitch. Oh! She became very angry, and her anger grew so much that she walked away and left me, to sing alone, or walk away. I stood there and finished my song, oh, everyone cheered. Since then I have build a wall of confidence, in myself, and in singing alone. Thanks to my partner. Don`t you agree with me?

So now after many years of singing in my own Country, I am now ready to leave home for some place I will be able to do better with my singing. For many years I have been dreaming about going to the United States, and so with some of the meager things of my life being done, I am now ready for this trial. It is very hard for West Indians to go to the United States, but I know that if God wanted me to go, I could do it.

To go to the United States permanently one must have a good bank account, have a good education, have a good career, be a good house-keeper, have someone who is sponsoring, go there as a student, and maybe after you finished, asked for permission to work in the country, marry someone who is a United States citizen, or permanent resident, and many other hard ways, or of course be rescued in, or work your way in illegally.

Well since I believe in doing the right things, as best as possible, I must go through one of the hard way. "My God is able, and so he did not let me wait too long. Soon I was ready to be on my way. My dear friend Grace must be commended for being such a help to me. She was with me from Montego Bay to Kingston and besides this, she was always there to give me words of encouragement. She is a wonderful person who is always ready to help, and lend a hand of mercy to those in need. May God continue to bless her, and may she never be weary in well doing. The last week came, and now I must say good-bye to my friends, and relatives whom I have grown to love over the years. I shall never forget the prayers, prayed for me by the Seventh Day Adventist Church members, as I left with the assurance that my God is able to keep me.

Like everyone else from another country America was my dream. America the land of freedom, beauty, opportunity and prosperity. The America that I dreamed of, was a land where the people are always happy. The houses were little cottages, surrounded by beautiful flowers gardens, a lawn, tennis court and large shady trees, with different kinds of birds flying from branch to branch. I thought all the people in America were dressed, in not expensive, but the most beautiful clothes, and that no one would ever dare to go dirty or not looking their best. I thought no poor people lived in America. I thought they were always loving and kind, as they appear to be, when they travel to other countries of the world. That in the United States more people were Christians, because they wanted to show their gratitude to God for the blessing he showered on them. Oh, I was so wrong. I did not realize that America was just another part of this wicked world blessed by God, and had the curse of sin and life problems, among the beauty, and blessing like every other place on the globe. I did not stop to think, that men suffer here, like every other place and even more so, because they are more blessed with opportunities, other countries would love to have for one day, God bless America.

GOD IS EVERYWHERE

I was sent to this country as a nurse and my application was accepted at one of the city`s well known hospitals before I came. I did not know that before you can work as a nurse you must have a license, or in those days a permit to work in the U.S.A. I was not told about this until I reported to the hospital the given day. Like thousands of foreigners, I had to go through the roughness of High School, even though these things had been done in my country, before coming here. Things are so different in this large city, so different from other countries of the world, but if you really want to make it, you must learn to agree, and fall in line with the strange customs. I soon found out that the grass is not always greener on the other side, but behind every mountain lies a plain, and the one who gets to the top of the hill, is the one who never gives up climbing. This city is a school, and any one who has a good school record here, if he or she is not lost in the hustle, and bustle, can become very successful, and will be able to make it any place else in the world.

With this in mind I have decided to forget every thing that ever happened, and to reach out for what was not yet done. Soon things began to fall into place, blessings began to fall on me. I was lucky then and even until this day my God never fails. This I can tell you freely, because in this city, where the pressure of life, and the enjoy of success, hard work, or unemployment can be read in the face of almost everyone you meet, a place where the fulfillment of nation against nation, where racial acts are sometimes like live fire, the black and white people alike were as nice to me, as I was to everyone. Without the help, and encouragement of many great people, who have helped me, I could never be successful this far. You may say, what success are you talking about? How much money do you have? I may even say none, for you see, for me success comes in many ways.

All these things I had in mind, but it was all a strange dream, for here was a country that was going to be destroyed like, everyone else and the people who lived in this country be destroyed if they do not turn from their sins, and repent and look to the living God. It was not until then, that I realize, how important it is, to look for a city, which has strong foundation, a city where no evil will come, where the builder and maker is God.

When I left Jamaica that day it was so nice and warm. When I landed at the U.S. airport three and a half hours later, it became cold. This was on the eleventh day of November and so half an hour later it began to snow. I had never seen snow before or had ever seen, or been in a city even half the size of New York. My dear friend Iris, who is like a sister to me, waited for me while she was on her vacation in Jamaica, so I would not be alone. I stayed with her then, and all went well. Soon I must learn to find my way around, to find a job, settle down, and do what I came here to do. I must say that even though New York is not what everyone from another country expected, we can help to make New Yorkers happy, and surely God is everywhere. "I love New York!" It is the only place in the world, where you can find so many things to do, places to go, and so much heights to gain, if you keep a steady head.

GOD`S GOODNESS

Many days I have tried to think, why God is so good to me, but though hard I have tried, I cannot comprehend. Great success came to me in the singing business, millions were not made but to me, being given the chance to sing, here was a great accomplishment. I am able to bring hope and some ray of happiness to many as I broadcast from the radio, and television each week. "My God is able to do great things, when so many people have it, or be able to do some of the things I can and is not able to do so. I love to share with others, show others that through lives road may seem so rough at times, there is always a bright side, if we just hold on until the clouds are passed away. Sometimes when I give a smile, someone who had been frowning for hours, would throw a smile back to me. When I started a conversation with someone, sometimes it is amazing how much they had to share with me. Tell me, haven`t you found that out? Maybe you could give it a try, if you had not done so.

NEW YORK

I am able to do things I really set out to do, and above all pressing forward to the prize of the high calling, in Christ Jesus.

In spite of our blessings and success, our days of trouble comes too, no one is free from trials, and it gives no warning. If it would from thick clouds, like when a storm is coming, we would have a chance to know it, but it do not. Maybe you have had your share and can agree with me, if not so you should make preparation, for some day, your day will come.

Neatris C. Mitchell

OUR DAY OF TROUBLE

After an interesting day we had to worship and went off to bed. Hoping to be well rested for the next day. At about 4 a.m. I was awakened by a sharp chest pain which prevented me from turning. I reached over and took two aspirins and soon I was again off to sleep. The clock alarmed letting me know it was 6 a.m. and now time to get ready for work. Oh, today was not going to be a working day for me, because as I tried to get up, I could not move. After awaking my husband and children, I was helped up but, the big surprise came when I found out my right hand was crippled. There was a severe pain which was preventing me from breathing, and keeping my hand in one position, resting on my chest. This pain goes from my elbow to my chest, to the middle of my back to the right side. They got me ready and I was rushed to the nearest hospital. Here they thought I was having a heart attack, but later found out it was Bursitis.

The doctor told me he would have to give me injections into my chest and shoulder and that it would take a long time for me to get well. It would also take three days per week of coming to the hospital for treatment. After four weeks of no improvement, I was told that now I do not only have to take injections, but would have to have surgery. I then decided to try everything first and then the surgery last. So I did exercise and used warm compress and visited the hospital three times per week soon I was on my way to recovery. While I waiting to recover, I had two car accidents in one month. For one of these accidents the doctor told me that someone should wake me every half an hour, when I go to sleep so as to make sure, that I would wake up and that even though my condition was such, and I was in so much pain, no medication could be given. In one of these accidents the only thing that was left of the car was the seat on which we were sitting. I do not know how we survived the crash, when the car was smashed beyond repair, excepting the guidance of the Angel of the Lord, in this we along with others could read clearly the mighty hand of God which saved my life for a purpose. For this may goodness to me, my life should belong to him, every moment that I live.

MY DAY OF ILLNESS

I went to sleep and asked that I sleep on. You see if it was time for me to die, I could have died in the car accident, that was my belief, and if it was time for me to die no one could save me. The pain I was feeling from the accident, was unbearable, but I could not be treated for it. When medication was given for the arm Indocin was induced. This medication should be taken for a few days and blood test should be done quite often, so as to see how this is affecting my blood count. This was done for quite a long time and so when the test was done, they found that my blood was down to nothing. The doctors told me I could fall dead, so I should not go anywhere by myself. At that time there were people waiting to see me, to be interviewed, to work with my husband so I had to leave.

The angel of the Lord encamped around them, that fear him and delivereth them. Surely this is what God did for me. Now that I am suppose to be dying from too low blood count, a blood clot above my left breast and battered tissues in my chest, bursitis in my neck going to my shoulder, down to my back, and three months of allergy, caused by eating and drinking chocolate, that causing my breathing to be almost completely stopped, was no easy way to stay alive. Many times I thought this was my last moment, but through it all, God kept me alive.

One day my doctor told me right away to see him. When I went, he did a routine check up, after the examination he found a tumor. I had no idea there was a tumor, but two weeks later I had to have a surgery. Soon all this was over, but the effects would be longer felt. It took me two years to feel like my old self and to return to work. Just before this happened, my husband and I jad just started a business, which cost us much more money than we thought it would. There were so many things that we

58

should have checked out, we did not do and because of this we had to pay a great price, this caused us all the trouble in the world, to get started and soon after starting it became a very successful business, but soon something went wrong, and before we knew it was all gone.

Because of my illness I had to stop working. My husband was now out of work too, for one year and six months. During this time my daughter started college and decided to live away from home. She was not able to get help because of my illness our tax paper were not as they should be. She was out of reach of getting a grant. My son is now doing well in school and became a popular student because of the achievements he has made and soon he had too many friends and I became fearful because some of these students are going in the wrong direction.

MY SON AND DAUGHTER ON GRADUATION DAY

My daughter in the front row and wearing a broad smile.

In some instances he would participate in activities of the senior, while he was just a junior. After his sister left for school he became very lonely and began to stay out more. He was now getting careless in his school work, now his father and I became very fearful and so we sent him away to private school. Since he was so advance in his school work, he was allowed to take his examination which saved him for years, and he was able to prepare for college three years earlier. The taking of this exam was his idea and he must be recommended for this. Many young people spend their time on sports only and in later years they really do need more schooling to survive. Sone of the leading people in some of today`s well known places, I am told some have hard jobs, reading, understanding and singing papers, so I would like to ask all young people to learn to read and write. Sometimes, one do wonder where the parents and teachers were when the children could use some help to make the right decision.

One should never forget that all we can hold on to is a good education and good character to make life worth while living. Life for him has changed suddenly, and this makes my family worried. We were not able to get any help from the city, or any other place. To see how hard we have worked, how honestly we try live, and to find that is only the hard working, and the honest people who suffer, was no fun to take.

This was a time for discouragement, but God`s children must be prepared for whatever comes and remember that although he slays me I will never doubt his mercies.

Sometimes it was very hard but, he was always there to help us. One day when the bills were checked, we needed fifteen hundred dollars and seventy five cents, there was not even one dime in the house. So I said to my husband we must pay the bills tomorrow dear, then he said if we wer5e not living here, we would have had money. So I told him that the same God lives here too. That evening as I checked the mail, sure enough the money came. As the tears rushed down my cheeks, I thought of how wonderful a God we serve.

Another day we had to come to the city, but we had no money for the gas or the toll. My husband thought I was crazy to ask him to drive the car out from the garage, but I know my God would provide. I forgot a letter with my appointment, so I went back to search for it, as I looked, I found an unopened letter. Yes, this had a check, it was quicky taken to the bank, it was cashed, and soon we were on our way. I could have told you more stories, but some other time.

He permits each of us to be tested and not more than we can bear. If we bear our testing faithfully we shall be greatly rewarded. My friends all I can tell you is that I my self is not able to understand it of myself, I can do nothing but I can do all things through Christ. No good thing will my God keep from me, if I love and serve him. "Surely my God is able."

MY FAMILY

While here in New York, I was privilege to work with many nice people, as a nurse in the hospital, homes or nursing homes. The people in the hospital in which I worked, are wonderful people. We share our joys, and sorrows, and do our best to make the sick as comfortable as possible. Without them my joys would be much less. In spite of life's success, my children's good grade in school, my husband getting a job, and being blessed with the greatest blessing of all, the greatest that one can ever have, a knowledge of Jesus Christ and his soon return. My husband like ninety-five percent of other West Indian men, was for a while very unhappy in this country. He would sit for awhile and compare the weather, the crimes, and many other things, that is not so easy for him to forget. You see in New York style of living is so different from the life style of other countries and namely the West Indies, and so different from what everyone from another country is expecting to find. In this world the children of God should never worry about the conditions that now exist in this world seeing, that the Bible told us that they would happen long ago.

Neatris C. Mitchell

**MARLENE ENJOYING SOME LONG
ISLAND BREEZE IN FRONT OF HER
HOUSE**

MARLENE AND HER ADOPTED DAUGHTER ON A CHRISTMAS EVE

As the years go by he can clearly say with me "God Bless America." There is no other country in the world like this one. This is the land where you can take nothing and make it into something. As God`s children here we have pledge to be good citizens, rendering the best service that we can give and caring for others. Then we should let it be known that we are looking for the holy city, whose builder and maker is God. Thank God that nothing that will make us unhappy will enter there.

My husband is a great guy, he is a very good husband and everything a child can expect from a father. My family and I are trying to make us the opportunities this country has to offer, and to prepare for what is ahead of us. Soon Major illness would strike, and threatens the future of my family. As a wife and mother, I always try to do my best for my family. To keep my home life in order at all times even though I have to work so hard. Maybe you think I am just trying to fool the crowd, but I must say that my wonderful family, and I work together. It is good tom have them in everyday. Through it all God is good to us, and his blessing never fails.

MY HUSBAND AND I

Mr. Reynolds: "Did you get an invitation A.I.B.G.A. to sing at a farewell Patry."

Castoria: "Oh yes, I got it sir, I don't believe your members would consider me, I just can`t believe it."

Paul: "We are lucky to have this special lady with us tonight, and at this time Miss Castoria will give us a solo."

Paul: "Who is this young lady? I would love to see her later."

Paul: "Hello, my name is Paul. I am visiting from the United States. I was invited to his party by a friend. I have enjoyed your singing, have you considered going abroad."

Castoria: "Not really, but maybe one of these days. I do not where to begin. It is very hard for us to go to the United States."

Castoria: "Nurse, how do one get to go to America?"

Nurse Bernard: "I don`t know but think you have to go to kingston and ask at the embassy."

Castoria: "I hope when I go, they will allow me to go to America."

David: "Today I got a package for you it is in the livingroom."

Castoria:	*(All excited)* "It is a record, made from the poem I sent to the U.S.A. come and listen to the sound."
David:	"Darling I love it, and the folks that heard it loves it too."
Castoria:	"I am going to try to go to America, if it is ok with you."
Castoria:	"Teacher, do you like this poem? I wrote it."
Teacher:	"May I read it."
Teacher:	(Reading silently) then in a loud burst she said "from which book did you write this?"
Castoria:	"I made it up myself, you see Mr. Brown, I love to write about the flowers, trees and people loving one another. Do you love that too.
Teacher:	"I do not encourage my student to lie." *(She said angrily)*
Castoria:	"I cannot believe so many people are trying to go to the U.S.A. Look how crowded this place is."

Embassy personnel "You must have a good bank statement, a trade, career, profession, be a good student there, be sponsored by a citizen or be given permission to work. Try to have a permanent stay, and boy, don`t be caught there illegally."

Castoria: "America is one of the richest counties, in the world. It must be so beautiful there? I will do everything to get there."

David: "What have you found out from the Embassy today? If you get to go there, you could stay for one year."

Castoria: "David! I have got the visa." *(Such excitement)*

David: "You must tell the church you are going to be leaving soon."

Castoria: "Oh! Cecilia! How come it is cold and the sun is shining? When will it snow? It must be beautiful then, boy! It is cold."

Cecilia: "Girl, the American dollar do not come easily. It takes hard work and careful planning."

Castoria: "Nothing that is good comes by easily. New York seem so different from what I thought. Maybe other foreigners will agree with me."

Cecilia:	"Well Castoria, if we can do it, you can do it too. All you have to do is give it a try."
Castoria	"Good morning, may I please see the director?"
Receptionist:	"Well she is very busy, I do not know if she can see you."
Castoria:	"I have an appointment with her, for today, please check to see if it is written in your book."
Director:	"Castoria, I am happy to see you, welcome to New York. Have you brought the papers for the nursing?"
Castoria:	"Sure, they are right here. Here they are."
Director:	"Oh, Castoria, you do not have the license or the permit."
Castoria:	"What is a license and a permit for? You see in my country we do not get a license to do nursing and even though I have received many letters from you, you have forgotten to mention it. What will I have to do?"
Director:	please send these forms to Albany, then you will have to do a short course and take the State Board Exam. Now you can work as a Nurses Aide."
Castoria:	"I will do what you told me, and I will be back to see you."

Mr. Clarke: "Castoria, early tomorrow we will go down town to try to find you a job, take your certificate, and papers received from the immigration. You need these things before you can work in this country."

Castoria: "I must get a job, until I pass my exam."

Cecilia: *(To her husband Mr. Clarke)* "How did you make out with Castoria today? Was she able to find a job?"

Mr. Clarke: "Honey, you know it is not so easy, everyone must have much experience and training. She will have to pack tomorrow they said. Sorry I will not be able to go with her. I hope she can find her way."

Castoria: "I will find my way, all I have to do is read well, and ask questions."

Cecilia: "How did you make out with the job hunting today?"

Castoria: "Pretty good. I will be starting in Great Neck tomorrow. I will be taking the Long Island Rail Road train from Penn Station."

Cecilia: "How will you get there? Where is this place?"

Castoria: "the place is called Long Island. They said it is real country like. It is nice all year round, even when it snows."

TWO PATIENT WITH WHOM I DID PRIVATE DUTY

Cecilia: "Castoria, when will you be going home, I heard you are leaving."

Castoria: "Next Thursday, the ladies that are working at home are not here now. One is sick and the other is on vacation. I must go for a short time and then return."

David: "Hello Castoria, the children and I are so happy to know that you could make it here to see us. One of the ladies went on vacation and the other one is out sick, my dear. I do hope you will be able to take us with you this time.

Uncle: "When are you going to the embassy?"

Castoria: "I was told by the immigration, that I will have you and the children in six weeks, so I must return to make preparation."

David: "What have you done about the recording? Will you be able to do it there? How soon?"

Castoria: "America is a wonderful place, I love it but everything takes time, but it is just not the way we foreigners thought of it. When I return, all these things will be taken care of. I am sure I will be able to do it well.

MY RETURN TO NEW YORK

Castoria: "Cecilia, my family is fine now, and they will be here soon girl. When they reach New York, I shall have to work in the hospital. For all I have heard about Columbia Presbyterian Hospital I would apply there."

Cecilia: "I am glad to have you back, those plans are great, give them a try."

Castoria: *(To her patient)* "My family sends their regards and hoping to see you soon. Even if I work elsewhere sometime in the future, you shall be one of my favorite patients."

Cecilia: "Since I made those applications to the embassy, and the hospital here, the hospital need you to call them, and your family got their visas. Good for you girl.

Castoria: "Cecilia, I have seen an advertisement in the News paper today and I would like to give it a try. I will be interviewed on Monday."

Cecilia: "What is the advertisement about?"

Castoria: "It is all a mistake. When you asked in your advertisement for voice I thought it was related to singing."

Manager: "You have a good background, so you never know, you will hear from us in two weeks. I think you have a good chance."

Castoria: "I went to 125th Street in Manhattan, today to seek an apartment but the landlord looked at me and said, Miss this apartment is not for you. Why would he say that? I also saw an advertisement with an apartment in Rockaway, I called and got an appointment, but when I went, they told me it was just rented. How could he have rented it, when he told me to come at 3 p.m.?"

Patient: "You have to be very careful in choosing where to live."

Castoria: "Cecilia, I have received a reply from the place where I did my interview in New Jersey. I will be working with a broadcasting station. I am so happy."

Cecilia: "Don't be too happy, your accent may get in the way."

Castoria: "I will not know unless I give it a try, with God all things are possible.

Castoria: "I just want to thank you for everything. I am sorry, that I have to go, but now that my family is here, I must go to work in a hospital."

Patient: "I am going to miss you Castoria. Miss you very much, but I am happy for you, and your family."

Castoria: "David let us go to the beach on Sunday."

David: "by the way Castoria, since there was another David in your life, why nut call me Albert sometimes? Lets use my middle name. That`s a great idea, we will go to the zoo, we must take pictures too."

Castroia: "Please read that for me. What is ti saying? By the way, please remember to call dad. Go on with the reading."

Albert: "This group will be singing at Grand Concourse temple and would like you to sing there."

Casroria: "What date is that going to be."

Daughter: "Let me see, it will be on Sunday ane month from now."

Castoria: "OK, I will accept the invitation."

Clerk: "Castoria, Frank would like to see you in his office. It is about working with the television."

Castoria: "Sure I will accept, sooner or later."

Radio Station Manager "Castoria, you have been doing well, would you consider television, radio or television."

Castoria: "I don`t know, this morning I found out that my daughter is very ill. I will have to be with her for a while. That is what I came to tell you."

Manager: "My God, I am sorry to hear about that."

Manager: "This is your big break, everyone wants this break, how can you throw it away? Give me an answer, for God sake."

Castoria: "I have none. Maybe five to ten years from now. I just don`t know. Goodbye Frank."

Castoria walked away from the office with her head hanging low in sorrow.

Albert: "how was your day Castoria?"

Castoria: "I was asked to work as a Show Producer with Television."

Albert: "That`s a big break for you, Castoria, will you accept?

Castoria: "as soon as the storm of sickness is over."

OUR HOME ON LONG ISLAND

Stan: "Mom did get you a record."

Castoria: "NO son I did not."

Stan: "Well, one is here for you. May I play it? It is your own record. Let's listen it.

Mr. Clarke: "My wife is having a party, please don't miss it."

Albert: "We will try you always have great parties."

Cislyn: "I miss you being in the Bronx."

Albert: "Why don't you come and spend a weekend with us? We are having some folks over next Sunday. We will play games, eat and have a good time. Since I am so busy, I can only see my friends like this once or twice per-year."

Cislyn: "See you on Sunday."

Castoria: Folks! We are happy to have each of you here today." We are hoping to have a wonderful time. I would like to tell you, that in spite of the many problems, we are blessed, and I will be starting a television show next

Madge: "Hi Castoria, how did you make out when you were sick?"

Castroia: "Well girl, it was real hard. Listen to this. When things got real hard, I went to the welfare office, and tried to get some help, just to pay the outstanding bills."

Madge: "How much of your bills were payed?"

Castoria: "What bills? I was told to bring a pile of papers, when the lady looked at them she said."

Lady: "Miss, you used to work for too much money."

Castoria: "What miss? I have been sick for more than two years, all that money is gone. If I had it, I would not be here."

Lady: "There is nothing we can do. If they decide to take away your home, we will put you and your family into a hotel, and put your things in storage."

Castoria: "Miss I had no business coming to you in the first place. I got very upset, I was wrong. I should not have said that, because the government cares.

Lady: "What do you mean?"

Castoria: "You see I am a child of God, and he owns everything in this world, and I should ask him for help and not you. God knows how to take care of his children."

Madge: "So, how did God help you?"

79

Castoria:	"I used hot water and rubbed with ointment, and exercise, that arm and girl I was back to work in no time. Surely my God is able."
Madge:	"Girl, that is some experience."
Castoria:	"girl sometimes like the job, we have lots of trials, but God has a way out. The government sometimes gives us help, but I went to the wrong worker."
Stan:	Mom & Dad, Marlene and I would like to be baptized."

As they all are around the dinner table, they waited for an answer from mom and dad

Mom:	"I am happy to hear you say that. This is the best choice both of you could ever make. This time more than any other time, you need to give your life to God, so that he can guide, and direct your path through life. The present pastor of the Grand concourse Temple, is the same minister who baptized me, when I was twelve years old. He was in Jamaica at that time.
Dad:	"I am happy for you and feel the same way, your mom do."

Stan Clover and Marlene

Baptismal service

Stan: "Mom and Dad, please attend parent teacher`s meeting on Thursday."

Dad: "Yes son, we will. What time are we expected to be there?"

Stan: "You should be there by 7:00p.m. so that you don't miss any part of it."

Dad: "I am very happy he is doing so well, seeing it is almost time for him to graduate."

Castoria: "That`s very good, his sister will be graduating in June, both of them will be finished not long from now."

Stan: "I am not feeling well. I must be taken to a doctor. I do not want to get sick now."

Doctor: "Your son must be admitted into the hospital to have some test done, so we can know what is wrong. I hope everything will be ok."

Castoria Retires

Castoria: "Mrs. Denis, who could give me some information on taking an early retirement?"

Mrs. Denis: "Please go to the union office and they will give you all the information."

Castoria: "Hi, I sure like what I heard at the office, Mrs. Denis."

Director: "We hate to see you go. Would you like a transfer for every weekend off?"

Castoria: "I have done twenty six and a half years of hospital service and nursing home, now, it is time to go out there, and use my knowledge to help others on the outside. Thanks for everything."

Co-worker   "I read an article about you in a paper yesterday. I did not know that you write, and record, broadcast on the Television, comes on the radio, and much more, and still work as a nurse, like all of us?"

Castoria   "I am only your co-worker and friend."

Castoria: "Dad, have you ever thought about changing your present line of work for something else."

Albert: "Why would you want me to do that?"

Castoria: "You have always been a waiter or a restaurant manager. Don`t you like the health field."

Albert: "I just don't understand why you would like me to change my job. I think that`s crazy."

Castoria: "You see if you want to do nursing you can do many more things. It is a wide field. We can use a lot of male workers and the pay is out of sight."

Albert: "I am going to take you up on that. Why not? If it is really so, I would like to give it a try."

MOM`S NEW JOB

Castoria: "dad, I have been granted a license to operate a Nurses Registry, this is just great. I shall do my best in finding the best workers who can give the best care.

Albert: "I wonder why my two children have to be sick."

Castoria: "Some things in life we may not have an answer for, but God knows best."

Albert: "You are right."

Castoria: "Lets hope the grand children will be ok, and by the way, our daughter will be giving us one soon. Things happen so fast, she grew up, got married now it is time for a baby."

Castoria: "So, Albert how do you like your new job?"

Albert: "I love it. I only wished I had started long ago."

Castoria: "See I told you. I knew you would love it."

Castoria: "Honey, nothing can be done before the appointed time."

Albert: "You are so right."

Cecilia: "How is your adopted granddaughter."

Albert: "After my daughter had her for two and a half years, a man claiming to be her father, caused a lot of problems so she gave the child to him. Now she is having her own child."

Cecilia: "Because of many problems, less children are being adopted."

Albert: "He had promised to kidnap, hurt, and destroy, everyone connected to this child."

Cecilia: "How is your son?"

Castoria: "He had a hard time, he cannot remember, what happened to them for a whole year. Thank God he is doing better now."

Cecilia: "Take good care of yourself, folks see each of you soon."

Nurse: "Marlene, you have got a girl *(as she held baby Chantel high in the air)* look how tiny she is. *(who was expecting a much bigger baby)*

THE TRIP OF LAST SUMMER

Two years after Shantel was born, my husband came up with an idea.

Albert: "Castoria let`s go to Jamaica this summer."

Castoria: "That`s a very good idea. When do we go? I am going to call you Bert for it is much shorter than Albert. You will like Bert better, don`t you ?"

Albert: "August will be a good time and that is when my vacation is due."

Castoria: "Sland and Sarah could go with us. I need to get away, I am so tired."

Marlene: "Dad told me you are going to Jamaica. I will be waiting my turn, as soon as you return I shall leave, and Chantel is going too."

Sland: "Are you taking me dad? I can hardly wait to get there."

Albert: "Jim the plane will be leaving at 9:00 p.m. what time will you be able to pick us up?"

Jim: "I will be there at 6:30 p.m. please be on the look out for me."

Sland: "Can we get a taxi now to take us to the hotel? So this is Montego Bay? Wow!!

Burt:	"Sure, we are now going to the Verney House Hotel."
Sland:	"I love this small hotel, the scenery and service is great."
Dad:	"Your mom and I have been coming here for many years."
Castoria:	"Oh, look at the mangoes, bananas and plantain. Look, the breadfruit are ready for the fire tomorrow, I shall have some with ackee and codfish."
Sland:	"At what time will we go to breakfast?"
Dad:	"Let us make it 8 o`clock so that we do not waste a minute of the time."
Chantel:	"It is nice here but I am tired, I want to sleep."*(baby)*
Castoria:	"So Sarah we will go to bed now."
Baby Chantel:	*(To waiter)* "May I have milk, eggs and toast?"
Waiter:	"Sure young lady."
Baby Chantel:	"Grandma, he said young lady."
Grandma:	"Yes dear, you are a young lady."
Sland:	"the food was out of sight. May we go to the beach."

Sland: "Wow, look at these they are beautiful, these girls, oh, they are beautiful."

Burt: "Oh such changes, look at these buildings! Not many countries produce such buildings."

Castoria: "Please leave us here and we will see you later. We are going to Dr. Cave beach."

Sland: "Hello, young lady on this island the ladies look so good. Oh, the way they dress is really eye catching. I hardly saw a fat girl. How do you stay so slim?"

Young lady: "Well, we eat fresh food, walk long distances to work, school or church for we do changing the buses so that they can have smaller ones."

Sland: "My name is Sland. What is yours? I was born here in this town but went to live in the States."

Young lady: "My name is Ruth, and it is nice meeting you. I wish you could take me to the States."

Sland: "Well Ruth, I hope to see you some more, maybe one of these days you will get to go to the States."

Burt: "Let's go folks we have lots of ground to cover."

Castoria:	"Many years ago, I wore uniform like yours. Girls, you are looking beautiful."
Burt:	"Sland here the parents pay a lot of attention to their children. Those parents work, and then take them home, walking long distances with them. They are not allowed in school without uniform either."
Castoria:	"How is school life for the children?" *(Castoria as she turned to ask a group of children who were about to share a piece of sugar cane among them were two mothers)*
Parent:	"Not so good at all Mam. We cannot get the books to buy for the children, we have to rent them, and when we get them to buy they cost a fortune. That`s why they work hard and so many get scholarship. We even have to make the benches for them to sit on. Yes, Mam."
Castoria:	"Most of the children do get a scholarship because they get such high marks. It is good that in spite of everything you can make good grades."
Sland:	"Why is it so hard for the children?"
Castoria:	"Oh boy, that`s real hard, but why is this, it was not like this before?"
Parent:	"When that country experienced a breakdown it suffers so much, that now every tact, and force, is needed to bring a

dead Island back, to life. Believe me it has made a great improvement."

Burt: "Taxi."

Taxi Driver: "Where to sir?"
Burt: "Number five Agate Lane, sir."

Driver: "That`s thirty dollars."

Brut: "You are kidding. You must be. You must remember that the thousands of foreigners that pour into this country they bring you wealth and prosperity yes, so do not kill the goose, or you will not get the eggs, and no eggs no chicken, right? So treat us good partner, so we can keep coming."

Sland: "It must be very hard for the natives to survive here."

Castoria: "But strange enough they do, and do so very well. Some of these people are very rich."

Dorothy: "Hello Castoria, how is life treating you, since you left the hospital to do your own business?"

Castoria: "Girl long time don`t see, things just going great."

Dorothy: "What is your business like?"

Castoria: "We supply nurses, home health aides, and house workers, companions, and attendant, to hospital, nursing homes and homes."

Dorothy: "That`s great, it is helping peoplein many ways."

Castoria: "Well that was exactly what I had in mind, helping people. I love every drop of it."

Dorothy: "Where do you find time to do all these things."

Castoria: "Oh how I wish I could find more hours in one day. I would take the rest for myself. How about that? I plan every minute well, making sure not to waste anytime."

Michael: "Hi! My name is Michael, I watch you every week on the television, I don`t believe you are right here."

Castoria: "I am happy to meet you too. Just keep on watching."

Dorothy: "So what other plans do you have for the future?"

A SURPRISE VISIT

Castoria: "I must do something to help the young people. They must learn to be independent men and women, to have an aim and work towards it. For all to hear I will have to write songs, and sing it to them, and to teach them something in every word I speak, and every movement that I make."

Dorothy: "That`s a good idea, I wish you luck, Castoria."

Castoria: "I have enjoyed this lunch, but we must go. Take good care of yourself, Dorothy until such time. Please give my regards to the others."

Castoria: "I hope we can make it up to the Great House today."

Chantel: "What is the Great House, Grandma?"

Castoria: "It is a true story about a witch who used to live there. It is called the White Witch of Rose Hall."

Chantel: "Take us there now."

Castoria: "What a surprise, when Aunt Glads saw us today."

Burt: "What a surprise, that`s the way to do it when you do not have to make any great preparation."

Aunt Gee: "So folks, how is New York?"

Burt: "Beautiful, has opportunities for everyone who needs it, but you must be in good health, be not selfish, have love in your heart and be prepare to work hard."

Castoria: "I wish some of these young people, with their mannerly qualities, the drive to gain a good education, to fulfil the great plans, they have made for the future, could get a chance."

Aunt Gee: "Well I hope one of these days, I will be able to join you. Now settle down everyone, and have some food, a good home cooked fish."

Sland: "I wish we could take some of the comforts, of this Island with us."

Chantel: "Grandma, I would love to go back to the beach."

Castoria: "Not for today again Chantel, you cannot do it all in one day. Of all the things, I wish I could take the beach with me.

"A DAY AT THE BEACH"

As the day grow older, I decided to enjoy the white sands of the beach, and to spend a long time in the water seeing that its kind, is not found too easily. The water was just the way I was hoping it would be. It was clear and warm. My husband, son and two and a half year old grand daughter was with me. My husband is an excellent swimmer at times he would go so far out in the deep, that I would become fearful. But after a while he would return with a grin on his face, and saying how much he is enjoying the water.

My granddaughter was now going to have her first sea bath and believe me she enjoyed it every drop of the beach session. That is the first time my son has decided to return to his native, in many years, it brought great excitement to see him gazed, steadfastly on the beautiful girls as they wonder to and from the beach. He then wondered off with a dark tall and slender young lady. Who was at the time wearing a large smile. He later told us he would like to see much more of her.

We then had some of the good old time, meat patties and cola champagne. Boy, they were expensive. We just could not see how the prices have reached such a great height, and the native managed to survive. The rate for us is five and a half dollar for one Jamaican dollar. My granddaughter wanted to run off and play with her grandfather while he was far out in the deep. Little did she know, she could be covered several time by this water. I had sit with her while she had a good time in this warm water. On this beach where natives, tourist, and even some long haired rastas who would give needed information to the visitors, while they enjoy the comfort that the island had to offer everyone.

The fresh fruits, vegetables, and food grown in the earth, were as fresh, and healthy looking as years gone by. The custard apple, nesberry, mangoes, breadfruit, ackee, yellow yam, sweet potatoes and cassava, oh what a taste. The food is just out of site, such mouth watering taste. This taste linger a long time after the food is gone. The manner of the children, connot be equaled in any other places, to which I have traveled. The parents must have put a deal of time and effort to cause them to develop such qualities, which help them to open the gate way to success.

The qualities possessed by these young, people is one that every parent would love to see their children have. The ones who will listen when spoken to, come when called, obey orders when given, make plans for the future, and work towards them to get a good education, the one that will fit them for a place in today's world, and make them ready for the world to come. As I watched these children work so hard to reach their goal, I could only wish that more young people, could use them as an example. That all the youth of the world could see how happy these young people are, and how they have so little, and yet so much.

Folks I must go visit my friends, and family and the brothers and sisters of the churches in and round the town, that I used to visit. It was time for excitement, meeting and greeting many folks. Many of the older and middle age folks who knew me well but the teenagers acted as though I was from a foreign country, and where my language was the only one spoken by its native.

The young people were so attractive, it was a pleasure to talk to them about the future. In spite of the hardship that is existing in the country, and the long search for employment. They had the future all mapped out, and so enjoy going to school even though it is a great sacrifice both for them as well as their parents.

The books needed for the opening in September, ran into hundred of dollars, for each child. Some parents had to rent then from the school, if they did not have the money to purchase them or if they could not be found in the stores.

Some of the parents had to pay for the benches that they had to sit on in school. You see when the country experienced a break down it suffer so much that every effort, force, and tact needed was being used to bring back life into an almost dead island. But because of the wise planning of the dedicated leaders, and the unselfish help of other countries, the country has made great improvement at this time.

Many of these young people set a very high standard and to reach them, they have to give it their all. Most of them have to walk long distances to, and from school, and at the end of each school year must pass their school exam with flying colors. The way they dress is really eye catching. Each school choose the colors and style of the children uniforms. They look so clean, neat, and beautiful, and the uniform is out of sight. Even though they are missing so much, they have so much to offer.

Togetherness, the parents, teachers and children work together to make school life worth while and educational goal reached.

Hard work do pay off because they were able to earn their daily bread and live in beautiful homes, such as were not easily found in most places. Such homes were not used as for family dwellings, but were also used as guest house than to stay in a hotel. One person said it makes her feel more at home. These foreigners that pour into the country by the thousands, each year bring wealth, and prosperity, to the uncomparable island. You see the payment for labor here is very low, when compared to that of many countries, of the world. If one plan, and work well, be unselfish, and hard working, he can build a prosperous life, and live independently.

The food of this island is always fresh and healthy. The milk has a rich tasty flavor, the meat is fresh at all times, and when cooked cause the mouth to water. One have to be able to control his appetite, because when served, never say when to stop. The prices are out of sight, so you have to be able to get much more for your dollars, depending on where you are living especially if you are coming from an American country. Sometimes you cannot help but wonder how the natives survive on the small pay they receive as wages. But strange enough they do. Most of them do so well, fresh and healthy but everywhere there is a loud cry for more money. No one mind spending, for everything is so good.

After enjoying our stay for three weeks, and no one enjoyed it better than our granddaughter, we were now ready to return to New York. We would again be greatly missed, by our relatives, and friends. Each person gave us their requests, we babe them goodbye. How I hate to leave behind the fresh fruits, vegetables, custard apple, mangoes, breadfruits, ackee and much more.

Castoria:	"Burt we must try get a flight for this Sunday."
Burt:	"We have a reservation for next Wednesday, why should we change it."
Castoria:	"I think we should leave even thiugh we are having a good time. I just feel we should go, we have a lot to do in New York, three weeks is good timing dad."
Sland:	"Let's ask the hotel owner to help us get a flight."
Hotel owner:	"Yes I will give it a try."
Castoria:	"Did you have any luck?"

Hotel owner: "Sure I got you a flight for Saturday."

Burt: "What Saturday? Doing our own business? Oh no."

Castoria: "If God permits us to get that flight, he must have a reason so let us travel honey."

Ticket clerk: "Ms. Castoria, your son cannot leave the country."

Castoria: "What, seem to be the problem?"

Ticket clerk: "They did not stamp his passport, so I am not sure he ever lived in the States."

FROM MONTEGO BAY

Burt: "So what do we do now, he must return today."

Ticket clerk: "You will have to return his green card, here on the tomorrow flight, and he can return on the same flight."

Castoria: "I have half an hour to go into town, and to be back on this plane. I must let them know that he cannot leave today."

Marlene: "Someone called from the Verney House Hotel, about Sland, they will take care of him and send you the bill, but please call them."

Castoria: "Well that is good news, now I don't have to worry. Thank God he is safe."

Marlene: "Why is that such a good news?"

Castoria: "This is what happen to us."

We had a reservation but wanted to travel one or two days earlier. All the travel services we went to, they were unable to find us a change of time, so we decided to travel on the first given date while talking to the owner of the hotel, about this he said he would try to get a earlier flight. After we left for down town that morning he was able to do as he promised, but the day he got for us on a Saturday, and according to the Bible we do not take pleasure trips on the Sabbath, My husband said oh no, never on a Saturday, but I turn and said to him that God who knows all do know that we do not travel on the Sabbath, and since he gave us the reservation he must have a reason for it. So we must go. You see if we are his children, he watches everything we do just like he does for everyone, but he directs the path of those who walks in his way. So my husband agreed and we were now ready to leave but you see life is never free of trouble, and the devil is always there, to make a mess of the good things God has done, and sure this time is no less. As we entered the airport to check out, we were told that our son could not leave with us.

You see he was sick for some years now and we would prefer to have him with us even though he can take care of himself. He had left his green card, given to him in the United States, so there was nothing was available, to prove that he was a resident of the United States, so when you travel make sure you have everything.

Now the clock was ticking away, letting me know I had half an hour to leave on that plane. I must return to down town Montego Bay, and leave his papers, explain what happened, and then return to the plane, that was now loading. This I told to the taxi driver, and off we went. The worst part of it, was that when I was ready for down town my son had already left, and now he was nowhere to be found. You see he was mad with us thinking, that we did not want to return with him. As we left the shore of Montego Bay, on that day, we could only hope that all would go well for him. I then tried to contact my daughter in New York to ask her to bring her brother`s green card, for him so that I could send it back on the plane on which I came. Seeing I could not reach her, I then decided to find out the fastest way for returning it to Jamaica the next morning. It took me two hours to get this information from the airline department, while I was checking every where and no one knows a passenger. Suddenly a passenger told me to go down stairs, she was right. They told me what to do and that it could go until the next morning.

When I returned the next day at eight a.m. I was told that I am too late the special delivery package had already left. I told the lady she just do not understand, then the man takes the special packages the plane, and came back to the desk, I ask him to run back to the plane for me and this would be his good deed for the day.

I wrote the paper quickly and he rushed off. They told me not to pay for it, until he return from the plane. I was sure the Lord would work things out for me, so I was not worried but as a human I was anxious for awhile. I must remember the kindness of those people.

I was then given a baggage number and told me to call the folks in Montego Bay and tell what this number is so that when my son get to the airport it could be easily given to him. I was calling the hotel where he was staying but the line always busy. This number could not be given, you see when we reached home we received a phone call that night telling us that my son had returned to the hotel where we were staying and that he would be taken to the airport by the person that took us there and that I should not worry. This brought great relief to us. We then went to the airport to meet him, the plane came and all the passengers came through customs but no sign of my son. We checked with information, but the computer showed that he was having some trouble. Still I encourage my husband to wait a while longer, which he did, but there was no sign of him. Now we must go home. As I turned around to leave, I felt a hand on my shoulder, as I turned to look to see who it was, I heard a voice saying, hi mom. It was my son.

The next morning there was a special broadcast from Jamaica. It had been badly hit by a hurricane, and many died, and thousands homeless, and some areas completely wiped out. When I could not get the telephone call through to Montego Bay, it was because the lines were down. I just could not come to believing how much interest the great

God of the Universe had in my family and I. How can I help but trust him.

Castoria:	"That morning I insisted on sending that card even though I was having a hard time, doing so."
Castoria:	"You must get this on the plane, you must."
Clerk:	"Miss you don't understand, it is too late."
Castoria:	"Sir, please try."
Baggage man:	"Ok, I will try. Please wait until I return."
Castoria:	"I will wait."
Baggage man	"I have made it, just before the door close."
Castoria:	"Thank you, you have made my day."
Sland:	"Hi mom, hi dad, it is good to be home."
Castoria:	"Thank God you are home."
Dad:	"I am happy to see you.:
Castoria:	"What a God we serve, his ways are always the best we should never question his doings."
Marlene:	"How would you manage with the baby, if you had stayed? This will be the worst hurricane to hit Jamaica."

THE HURRICANE

This hurricane was the worst in the history of this island, and they have had some bad ones, so they had nothing to eat or wear. Thousands of the beautiful homes I told you about were gone. The people in the other countries were now sending everything they could to save lives and help the devastated island. Sometimes we as human being do not see how much caring other people have in them until they need help. It was amazing to see how much help was given to them by so many tribes and nations of this world.

One week later I received words from my relatives they were small looser of property but no loss of life. I was not satisfied with myself in that I had not gone home to bring them some food, and clothes so I did just that. I could not believe what I saw, I asked myself where did the Jamaica of three weeks ago went?

The hotel in which we were staying was badly damage. Not a cracker or a cookie for the kids, for the flour mill was destroyed. I saw Jamaica the land of food, having nothing like food. Yes, nothing like food, life is so uncertain. I was able to get two bread, this was able to share for many families too, for there was nothing to buy.

This time I spent only enough to help others. My home had only sustained a leak from the hurricane. As I returned to New York, the one thing that could not leave my mind, was that God is able. For his goodness, I will never be able to repay him. He must take my life and let me use it to his glory and to help others.

Castoria:	"The God we serve knows everything. He has a plan for everyone. He knows the end from the beginning. Marlene, it is good to know him."
Marlene:	"Come listen to this everyone, thousands of homes are lost, many lives too, and communications are cut off. You just missed it."
Castoria:	"I must return to help the people with food and clothes as soon as I can get a flight. In the mean time, I must help with emergency supply."
Castoria:	"I just cannot believe that this is the same place with everything so beautiful."
Albert:	"I must say thanks to God, who made us, and the heavens and earth. He knows the

end from the beginning, and he always protects me."

AMERICA

CASTORIA
(speaking to someone who is new in America)

This is the land where you can do good in life or you can make a fool of yourself.

LADY
Why do you say that?

CASTORIA
When you reach the United States you must be serious about life. You must have a trade, skill or a profession. You need for your training here, or in your country, a licensed piece of paper, to show what you can do. Abide by the laws of the country, and do what is right.

CASTORIA
By the way what is your name?

LADY
My name is Mary

CASTORIA
Mary do you have a Green Card?
Reference and Diplomas?

MARY
Yes miss. I have.

CASTORIA
What were you trained for?
How many years experience do you have?

MARY

I have my things for all that you said

CASTORIA

Another thing I must tell you, is that you will need to go to school here, no matter how education you came here with, because it is different here.

SCENE: Mary and Castoria walking along down Gunhill road. Going from Boston Post Road to White Plains Road.

CASTORIA
(to Mary)

When you work do not be fooled by the dollars. Make sure you put them to a good use.

Today you have it, but if you lose it, it will be as if you never worked a day in your life.

MARY

This is a wealthy country so how can you lose it all?

CASTORIA

Well Mary sometimes things are not what they seem

When you need a penny or a nickel and you have no place to get it from it is not a joke. Take it from me I have been there

MARY

I did not get your name

CASTORIA
Get yourself good Health Insurance. Save your money in a Mutual Funds and Stock and Bonds. So it can multiply to make your life comfortable.

"MY VACATION AFTER THE HURRICANE"

(SCENES OF FLASH-BACKS DAYS AFTER THE HURRICANE)

CASTORIA
David I would like to go to Jamaica to see how it is now. I am told that things are looking good there.
What do you think David?

DAVID
Well Castoria that is a great idea, but I will not be able to go with you at this time.
Take some time off I will stay here.

CASTORIA
(Talking to a friend)

Hello how are you?
I was hoping I would see you.

FRIEND
I called you two days ago, but you were out.

CASTORIA
I will be going to Jamaica in a couple of weeks, would you like to go with me?

You said I should let you know when I am going back there.

FRIEND
Sure Castoria! That would be great
I hope I will be able to take that time off.

CASTORIA
David!   My friend that was here yesterday would like to go to Jamaica with me.

DAVID
That is a great idea.
You will have company

FRIEND
Now I will go and speak to my husband to see if I can have that time off.

FRIEND TO HER HUSBAND
Hello honey! My friend Castoria is planning to go to Jamaica in two weeks, I would love to go, if it is possible.

FRIEND`S HUSBAND
We will be able to manage for two weeks.
Take the time and go.

FRIEND
Castoria I have gotten the time off,
so I will be going with you.

CASTORIA
Great! Now I can make the reservation.
I know we will have a good time.

**(SCENE OF CASTORIA AND FRIEND
LEAVING FOR JAMAICA FROM JFK
AIRPORT)**

**SCENE WITH FRIEND AND
CASTORIA TRAVELING FROM
MONTEGO BAY TO HOTEL**

CASTORIA
We would like to go to the hotel that is right in
front of Doctor`s Cave Beach

DRIVER
Sure! No problem ladies.
They were the ones who asked me to come and
get you

CASTORIA
Yes sir! Thank you.

FRIEND

So how is Jamaica now since it was struck by the hurricane?

DRIVER
Well as you can see there is great improvement man. Larger and more beautiful homes have been going up everywhere.

Prices have sky rocked.

Tourist trade is blooming.

Nature have given a greater share of its blessing to the vegetation, and forest alike.

CASTORIA
It is wonderful how the Lord can take care of his people

(SCENE)

DRIVER
The driver reaches the hotel.
He unloads the luggage in front of the hotel.

FRIEND
This is just beautiful here.

CASTORIA
Yes! It is beautiful here.

The reason why I have chosen this hotel it because it is much easier to get transportation from here to all parts of the island.

FRIEND
That`s an excellent idea.

For transportation here, I am told that is most expensive for foreigners.

CASTORIA
Not only transportation my dear, but just about everything.

They have to try to make up for the loss.

Who cares about the cost when you do enjoy the worth?

(SCENE OF HOTEL REGISTRATION)

BUS BOY
Welcome! Please come this way ladies.

He took us to the front desk to be registered, while he carries two bags.

CLERK
Welcome! Let me get you started so that you can fell better.

She gave us information, booklet and our keys to our room.

BUS BOY
Takes our luggage to our room as he leads the way.

(SCENE)
Ladies looking at the view from the balcony.

FRIEND
Csatoria! Are you going for a walk after we eat
and change, or are we going to get some rest first?

CASTORIA
We will go for a walk right after we change.

FRIEND
Yes! Yes! I want to enjoy every drop of it here.
Every drop of the beauty.

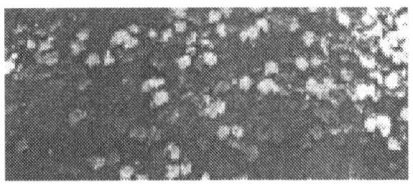

CASTORIA
I will do no business or visiting of family or
friends this time.

I am here for a complete vacation.

I shall see this island as I have never seen it
before.

SCENE: Registration with Tour Bus Company

CASTORIA & FRIEND

Looking at pictures while waiting to be registered.

They are amazed at the pictures of places they saw, and most eager to get there.

TOUR COMPANY CLERK
Welcome! How may I help you?

FRIEND
We would like to register with you if we can.
We were told that your service is great.

CLERK
Thank you.
We are ready to leave at 9:00 a.m. each day, and we are back by 5:00 or 6:00 p.m.

CASTORIA
That sounds very good.
So we will register with you for the length of our stay.

SCENE: Tour Bus Loaded at 9:00 a.m. to leave for the North Coast. (St. Ann)

TOUR GUIDE ANNOUNCES
We will be stopping at such places as-the Run-A-Way Bay Cave, Discovery Bay,
Firn Gully, and Dunns River Falls.

FRIEND
Castoria! What beauty! It is awesome.
I am amazing to see how the transport works.
How at the other site we saw all these Ancient
Equipment used by the sponsors years ago.
It is unable

CASTORIA
Do you know I have been in this area so many
times, year after year, but believe it or not, I have
never climb to the top of the fall before today.

I usually only stay by the beach. It is so good
to climb to the top of this fall.

"SCENE FROM TOP OF FALL"

TOUR BUS DRIVER

If you have gotten your pictures, and all the
things that you need, we can leave now.

FRIEND
I am really having a good time.
It is great to be here with you Castoria.

SCENE OF TOUR BUS RETURNING TO MONTEGO BAY.

CASTORIA TO FRIEND
We have to have an early breakfast
today, so we can leave early.

SCENE OF TOUR BUS GOING TOWARD THE DEEP WATER PIER, ON IT`S WAY TO HANOVER.

CASTORIA
When I am at my home in Glendevon
I can see this Pier clearly.

It has the most beautiful scenery in the night
when the ships are lighted and are leaving and
coming in.

When I was living here, it was not so built up
around the pier. I could never dream all these
places of business in the area.

It is wonderful to see the great development.

FRIEND TO CASTORIA
On our way back, I do hope they will stop at the
food market you told me about, so that we can get
some fruits.

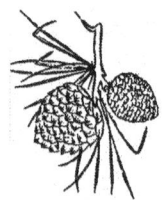

CASTORIA

Look! At the fruit trees along the way, they are loaded with fruits.

Oh! The new growth is contributing to this.

More people are working now because they are helping to rebuild.

Everything is just beautiful.

FRIEND

Did you hear where we are going after we leave the pier?

CASTORIA

No.

FRIEND

They said we will be going to this river where we can ride on a raft.

CASTORIA

I can hardly wait

CASTORIA & FRIEND

Walking toward the restaurant as the bus stops. Both eating lunch.

TOUR BUS

Reloaded and on it`s way.

Both gazing at the scenery along the way.

Passing farms with animals, people on their way to work, market, and other places.

SCENES OF TOUR BUS UNLOADING SO THAT PASSENGERS CAN GO TO THE RIVER FOR A RIDE ON RAFT.

People waiting at entrance with things for sale to tourist.

A man is seen climbing a coconut tree, so passengers can get coconut water, and jelly coconut.

CASTORIA & FRIEND
Purchasing Bammy and fried fish.

Passengers were guided to raft, as two by two they went for their ride.

CASTORIA & FRIEND
Drinking coconut water after their ride on the raft was finish.

CASTORIA
When will we be going to the farm that you told us about?

DRIVER
Just as soon as we leave from here.
They have a hotel there also. It is always full with tourist.

CASTORIA
Thank you.

SCENE OF TOUR BUS PASSENGERS UNLOADING IN FRONT OF THE HOTEL BY THE WAY TO THE FARM.

PASSENGERS ON FARM
Looking on animals and birds.

FRIEND
I thought we would have another day.
This is great.

DRIVER
No! Since it is so close by the river, we can just do it today. You are going to love every moment of it here.

CASTORIA
There are so many different kinds of animals and birds here, but the one I am happy to look at up close, is the island crow. It is a large black bird with long red neck, that looks like that of a turkey.

I never had a chance to see it up close to get a good view of it before today.

I am lucky to see one sitting on a branch close by.

They feed on carcass.

How about the animals that do the tricks?

Can we see them today?

CASTORIA TO FRIEND
The owner of this farm has a brother who is a friend of mine, he has a business on
White Plains Road, in New York City.

FRIEND TO CASTORIA
It is just a pity days like this must come to an end.

TOUR BUS GUIDE
Well folks, we must be going now.
I hope everyone is having a wonderful time.

FRIEND
It is now 5:15 p.m. we have reached our hotel back in town.

We have spent an indescribable day of beauty.

FRIEND
I cannot wait for tomorrow to come.

Let us go for a walk after dinner, and then get a good sleep, and be ready for all that tomorrow has to offer.

TOUR BUS
"GOING TO NEW CITY SITE SCENE"

SCENE OF ANCIENT WATER WHEEL THAT IS STILL WORKING.

Pictures are taken with 2 Native who gives information, and tourist give fees.

TOUR BUS GUIDE

We are now at a new city site, where we will have a chance to enjoy a lot of things

Such as:

"SCENES OF A BEAUTIFUL CITY SITE"
   a) New City Site
   b) Scene of Beach Site
   c) Scene of Under Water Boat Ride
   d) Scene of Band Playing
   e) Scene of Peddlers Selling Sea Shell and
      Ornaments.

FRIEND & CASTORIA

Taking pictures along the way of things they liked most.

We had a wonderful time here, and we are now on our way back home.

SCENES

TOUR BUS GOING TO FOOD-MARKET

Passengers unloading to purchasing what they need.

CASTORIA
I need a lot of fruits to take home
I want to eat many mangoes, nesberries, sweet sops, and many more fruits.

FRIEND
How can we eat all these fruits Castoria, girl.

CASTORIA
We will see how many we can eat when we get home.

FRIEND AND CASTORIA
They had dinner, fruits, and a good night sleep.

SCENE OF DOCTOR CAVE BEACH

CASTORIA & FRIEND
On the beach which was located just across from the hotel where Castoria and friend are staying.

They saw other people from the US and Canada.

They chatted with for a while and played in the in sand, before going into the water.

They decided to stay close to the hotel today and be ready for the street party later.

SCENE OF STREET PARTY "CLOSE BY"

    (a) Folks dancing
    (b) Calypso dancing and music
    (c) Limbo dancing
    (d) Groups singing island songs
    (e) Gift shops and sellers along the way
    (f) Buyers purchasing from Curio sellers

SCENE WITH CASTORIA AND FRIEND

Walking with other friends along the beach in the hotel area.

Castoria shows her friend where the old hospital was located, and tours of the hospital.

She then ask the others to sit and wait to view the ocean and the beautiful sunset.

FRIEND

Now shall we return to the hotel?

It is getting late for supper, and this part of the party is over.

I am going to bed early tonight, we have a long day tomorrow.

CASTORIA

After supper I will look at TV for a while have some fruits, and go off to sleep.

(BREAKFAST SCENE)

FRIEND

What will we be having for breakfast today?

CASTORIA

I am going to have some calaloo, codfish, boiled banana, fry plantains, and two fry dumplings.

FRIEND
What is the name of that fruit again?
The one that can be roasted.

CASTORIA
(Making a light laugh) O.K. it is called breadfruit.

That's good with ackee and codfish.
FRIEND
Yes! That is what I will have with some of that cocoa tea.

FRIEND & CASTORIA
Went to their favorite little restaurant for breakfast.

They usually sit outside to eat, so that they can see the folks go by.

CASTORIA
I really enjoy my breakfast.
How about you?
Girl don't even ask, it is so good.

SCENE

HOTEL LOBBY

Friend and Castoria met the hotel manager in the lobby.

MANAGER

I would love to have dinner with you ladies if you are free.

FRIEND

We can make ourselves free for your sake sir.

MANAGER

Should I consider that a yes?

CASTORIA

I believe so.

MANAGER

Ok ladies see you at 7:00 p.m.

CASTORIA

Are you ready for us to go shopping?

FRIEND

Sure lets go.

CASTORIA & FRIEND

We walked from fourth street, this is one of the Main Street in Montego Bay.

Castoria showed her where she met David her husband the first day.

There are changes such as a longer area of beach front, and a larger street.

CASTORIA

Our first stop should be the Curio Shop.

Here we will get a hat and basket, and something to take back for the girls in our office.

Then we will go to the store.

Then the dress shop at the center.

That should be enough.

"DINNER SCENE"

After a day of shopping we went back to the hotel and got dressed for dinner with the manager.

CASTORIA

Castoria all dressed up.

FRIEND

All dressed up.

MANAGER

Thanks for coming ladies.

We made some special dishes for you.

Tonight I hope you will enjoy some.

CASTORIA
Thanks for having us here.

MANAGER
Where in New York are you living?

FRIEND
We live in the Bronx.
Have you ever been to New York?

MANAGER
Yes! I have been there twice.

FRIEND
Did you have a good time?

MANAGER
Well I did not, because I hardly knew anyone at the time, I was alone during that time.

CASTORIA
Well the next time let us know when you are coming, so we can see you, therefore you would not have to spend your time alone.

MANAGER
Do you come to Jamaica often?

FRIEND
This is my first time coming here.
You see I own a business, so it is not easy to get the time off.

CASTORIA
Well I come here sometimes three or four times per week.

Sometimes it is business.

I have homes here and also some relatives.

I have business too, so when I come here, sometimes I can only spend a few days, or if

I am taking some time off with my husband.

MANAGER

Please let me know when you are coming and I hope you will come to stay here.

FRIEND

You do the same.

CASTORIA

Thanks for a wonderful dinner, and a great evening.

(DISCUSSIONS)

CASTORIA AND FRIEND

FRIEND

He had the most special dishes prepared for us at this dinner.

CASTORIA

I would love to do this another time.

Come on now.

Let us go and get our sleep.

Tomorrow will be a busy day.

We will be going to that special beach.

The tour guide said.

"SCENE OF TOUR BUS WITH ITS PASSENGER"

TOUR GUIDE
(Makes announcement)

Well folks we are on our way to the Negril Beach, where you will have miles of white sands, dishes of many kinds, entertainment, and many surprises.

It is a long way from here that is why we are leaving so early.

FRIEND TO CASTORIA
Look at the homes how beautiful they are.

CASTORIA
They are larger, and much more beautiful than before.

It is as if nothing ever happen to this place.
Everything is so beautiful.

"SCENE OF THE NEGRIL BEACH"

TOUR BUS
Passengers unloading from bus.

BEACH SCENE
People bathing, walking on the beach, taking pictures, and everyone seem to be having a good time.

CASTORIA & FRIENDS
Meeting other people from New York.
They came on other tour buses.
Castoria, friend, and new friends, are taking pictures.

CASTORIA
I would love to have some lunch at this time.
Let`s find a place to get some food.

FRIEND FROM NEW YORK
Let us go to an outside restaurant that a friend told us about.
It is close by.

RESTAURANT SCENE
Group seated and enjoying lunch, which consist of yellow yam, green banana, jerk chicken, fish, rice and peas, and curry goat.

Drink consist of cola champagne, and cola.

"BACK TO THE BEACH SCENE"

SEE BATHING AND BOATING SCENE

EVENING SCENE

All are invited to the entertainment area to enjoy the West Body Moving Music, off the cliff diving, and for the watching of the glowing sunset.

CASTORIA & FRIEND

Just to watch this diving looks dangerous to me. People would leap from an exceeding height to such distance below. It is scary.

FRIEND

I turn my head aside when someone is going to leap. Hoping no one would hit himself on a rock, because I do not believe he would live.

This was like nothing to the people who are doing this leap.

"THE SUNSET SCENE"

CASTORIA

It is time for the "sunset watch".
Look at how quiet everyone is.
Just waiting to see the last rays of the
Everyone has their camera ready.
The music stopped.
The sun in all its beauty as if with a
on its face gave its blazing splendor.
This is awesome, it is amazing.
It is beautiful.
The day is a complete one.

CASTORIA TO FRIEND

The most wonderful played, body moving music again sounded, and folks began moving about.

Some to get more drinks, some to dance, and some like us prepare to leave to different parts of the island.

FRIEND

No one will ever forget the time that was spent at the Negril Beach on that day.

That day the bags were packed, and we were ready for our usual routine.

Back from a well spent vacation.

CASTORIA

All good things at time do change and sometimes even come to an end.

So with this in mind, Castoria and her friend are ready to return to New York, feeling all refreshed and ready to get back to their every day routine.

FRIEND

I am so excited Castoria, about this wonderful time which we have spent together.

I am going to be planning for next year`s trip, as soon as I return to New York.

CASTROIA

I wish it was possible to have all the people we have as friends, travel with us when we return to Jamaica.

FRIEND

I am so sorry it is not possible.

One thing you could do Castoria, is to make a movie that others who are not able to come, can see how beautiful a place it is.

CASTORIA
Even the whole world would get a chance to see.

I think that`s a great idea.

FRIEND
Are you serious Castoria?

CASTORIA
This movie will tell my whole life story.

How everyone do have a chance to be the person they want to be and reach their goal by God`s grace.

FRIEND
That will be a very hard job Castoria.

CASTORIA
So is growing up in Jamaica.
God Bless America.

DISCUSSION SCENE
(between David and Castoria)

DAVID
Now Castoira with vacation and the storm behind us, let us move on to other things Darling.

CASTORIA

Jamaica is a wonderful place. I would like more people to know more about it, and of how good God is.

SCENE OF MOVIE SCRIP
(In the book form)

Group leaving from Kennedy Airport, to make movie part of which will be done in Jamaica.

SCENE: crew Landed at Montego Bay Airport, To do scenes up to point of coming to N.Y. to sing.

SCENE: Crew Return to New York.
AIRPORT SCENE: To do all New York Scenes.

SCENE: Crew now ready to do the other part of movie here in New York.

SCENE OF CREW: Celebrating the finishing of movie in New York with dinner at Castoria`s home.

Neatris C. Mitchell

DOING MY PART

I have tried my best in what ever way I can, to help my fellow black men and white alike, and in turn blacks and whites alike has done the same for me, and have been very helpful to me. Truly every human being that has ever lived is created by the true and living God. The creator of heaven and earth. Now after looking over the years I can say "Thanks to God for what I have accomplished in this world. You may say ah, she has not done much, but to me I have come a long way. If it was not for the grace of God, I would cause you to spit at me by the side of the street, but instead you can see and hear me even in your home, and greater will be when we meet in the kingdom of God. Oh, I ask myself what does it all amounts to? Well you are right, not much. Surely the answer comes back, not much.

Life hardest battle is to find a place it the world to come. My God who sent his son to die for all the one who has helped my hands to find something to do, the same God whose love stands fast forever and ever and to everyone that believes in him, this God is able. This God is able to keep me until the day arise, and the king of king descend to claim his own, those who have loved him and keep his commandments, shall live with him forever and ever.

I have learned to love him not because he has kept me in this world as a human being but because he has loved me from before the foundation of the world. I love him because he has given everything possible for the saving of my soul, which is so sinful. Yes, I love him because he adopted me into the greatest royal family that has ever lived. I love him, because he alone could have paid the price of the heavenly mansion for me. Yes, I love him because he has all the protection to keep me until the day of his appearing. I love him for some day soon, he will come again to take me away from this world where there will be no more troubles, sickness, crying or death. I love him because he gave his life on calvary's cross for me. Yes, I love him for he is able to open and close all doors. My God is able.

Sland: "Describe what you saw when you went to Jamaica."

Castoria: "They have no food, some lost everything it could of been worst."

Sarah: "Grandma, please tell me a story."

Castoria: "God made us and gave us all good things, he keeps using this world like apples of his eyes. Someday soon he is coming to take us to live with him if we do his will and if we do not we shall be destroyed. He is able to keep us until that day, Glory Hallelujah."

Castoria   "My God is able to keep me, He has adopted me into the greatest royal family, he is coming back again, oh, Lord thou art wonderful."

Oh, Lord thou art wonderful, how can I comprehend? We are in thine image Lord, thou has given us our birth. If I write, my pen falter, if I speak my tongue fail, but naught can thy wonders alter so to thee Lord I hail. Oh, Lord, thou art wonderful, thou art formed the earth, we are in thy image Lord, thou hast given us our birth.

Neatris Mitchell

**From Jamaica
To The United States**

THE OPEN DOOR

MONTEGO BAY

FROM

NEW YORK

ABOUT THE AUTHOR

Neatris C. Mitchell was born on the island of Jamaica, the West Indies, and she has fancied herself a writer, songstress, and radio and television host along with enjoying many other creative outlets. She has been these things and more, serving as a teacher and as a nurse for many years since coming to the United States and becoming a naturalized citizen. She continues to write and sing.

The author received the 1990-1991 Award for Nursing from "Who's Who in American Nursing," located in Washington, D.C., and she has worked with the New York Community finding jobs for many in the health care field. A Seventh Day Adventist, Ms. Mitchell has been a member of the Grand Concourse Temple in the Bronx, New York. She has also done over ten years of radio and ten years of television broadcasting in and for the New York Health and Community Service Organizations, in talent, greeting and talk shows.

The author was married for over thirty-three years, and has two grown children, two grandchildren and currently makes her home in New York City when not in Florida.

This is the author's first published book.

www.ingramcontent.com/pod-product-compliance
Lightning Source LLC
Chambersburg PA
CBHW020443290526
45785CB00002B/993